D1427977

CULTS AND ISMS

CULTS AND ISMS

by

J. OSWALD SANDERS

Consulting Director, Overseas Missionary Fellowship

Formerly issued as

HERESIES AND CULTS

LAKELAND
116 BAKER STREET
LONDON W1M 2BB

Copyright © J. Oswald Sanders 1948
Reprinted 1950, 1953, 1954, 1956, 1957, 1960 and 1961

Revised edition © 1962
Reprinted 1963
Reprinted 1966
Lakeland edition 1969
Reprinted 1971
Reprinted 1973
Reprinted 1974

ISBN 0 551 00458 4

PRINTED IN GREAT BRITAIN BY
LOWE AND BRYDONE (PRINTERS) LIMITED, THETFORD, NORFOLK

PREFACE TO FIRST EDITION

THE substance of these chapters was originally delivered as a series of lectures to the students of the New Zealand Bible Training Institute in the course of their studies in Apologetics. They were later reproduced in *The Reaper*, the magazine of the Institute, and in their printed form were used to deliver some from the clutches of the cults here treated. After revision, we have ventured to reproduce these studies in book form, in the hope that wider usefulness may be found for them.

Jude the Apostle gives abundant warrant for such an approach as is here used. "Beloved," he wrote, "while I was giving all diligence to write unto you of our common salvation, I was constrained to write unto you exhorting you to contend earnestly for the faith once for all delivered unto the saints," giving as the reason for his exhortation that "certain men had crept in privily . . . denying our only Master and Lord, Jesus Christ." The same reason has compelled the author to compile these studies.

The spate of subtle propaganda which comes over the air on the various radio networks, has strengthened the conviction that it is incumbent on Evangelicals, not only to indoctrinate their own members, but to raise a warning voice against the insidious encroachments of these Satanic counterfeits of true religion. Too long have we allowed the cults to win by default.

Numerous books, pamphlets and magazine articles from the pen of both antagonists and protagonists of the various heresies have been read and drawn upon in the course of preparation of these pages, for all of which the author gratefully acknowledges his indebtedness. Special mention must be made of *Chaos of the Cults*, by J. K. Van Baalen which he would recommend as the best book on the subject he has read; *Heresies Exposed*, by W. C. Irvine; *Confusion of Tongues*, by C. W. Ferguson; *Isms, New and Old*, by Julius Bodensieck; and *Some Latter-Day Religions*, by G. H. Combs.

The method adopted is simple and adapted to the purpose in view, viz. to enable ordinary Christians to resist the blandishments and refute the errors of these cults. It has been the aim throughout to quote from authorised publications of the cult under review, giving book and page, wherever possible, so that no injustice may be done. In cases where the original books were not available for research, quotations from them by reliable authorities have been given.

May the Lord Whose honour this book seeks to defend, bless it to the enlightenment of some and the emancipation of others of its readers.

J. OSWALD SANDERS.

Melbourne, Victoria.

PREFACE TO EIGHTH REVISED AND ENLARGED EDITION

SINCE this volume was first published, there has been a considerable shift in some of the cults under review, and a revision is more than overdue. Over the years some inaccuracies have been pointed out, and these have been corrected. If the views of any of the cults treated have been misrepresented, it has been unintentional. Every endeavour has been made to present their views fairly, preferably from their own authoritative statements. Statistics and developments within the various movements have been brought up to date. The treatment of some of the especially aggressive cults of today has been expanded and considerable new material introduced. A brief summary of some of the less-known cults has been added, to give readers at least an indication of their nature.

Some of the movements under review can hardly be classed as heresies—"opinions opposed to the commonly received doctrine, and tending to division and dissension." But they do come under the classification of cults—"great devotion to a person, idea or thing, especially such devotion viewed as a sort of intellectual fad." Among these the author would include British-Israelism, Freemasonry and the Healing Movement.

In view of a recent definitive doctrinal statement by Seventh-day Adventist leaders in which they affirm their adherence to the main fundamental doctrines of the evangelical faith, it would perhaps be unfair to include them under the term "heresy." But they still embrace sufficient doctrine unacceptable to evangelical Christians, and exercise such a divisive influence, as to preclude their being omitted from a book of this nature.

If the perusal of these pages delivers some from falling into error, and constrains others to emulate the Bereans, "who searched the Scriptures daily, whether these things were so," then the rather distasteful task of discussing the errors and aberrations of the cults will have been worth-while.

J. OSWALD SANDERS.

CONTENTS

INTRODUCTION

THE rise and development of the heresies current throughout the world to-day, constitute one of the most remarkable features of contemporary religious history. The nature of their teachings, and the rapidity with which each in turn has gathered a not inconsiderable following, are at once an evidence of the inadequacy of the teaching in the orthodox churches, and a vindication of St. Paul's prophetic utterance:

"The Spirit expressly warns us that in the latter times some shall revolt from the faith; they will give heed to deluding spirits, and to doctrines devil-taught, trapped by the hypocrisy of liars whose consciences are seared."—I Tim. 4:1-2 (Way).

In presenting "the case for the cults," Gerald E. Richter makes a challenging statement to which we must reluctantly give our assent. "Some phases of the 'cults' operations," he writes, "might well be emulated by their non-productive critics. They believe strongly in what they profess. They sacrifice of their slender means to a far greater degree than the more prosperous members of more orthodox faiths. They publish literature expounding their views literally by the ton, and devote hours, days, weeks of gratuitous service in its circulation, that others may be told and share with them the satisfying experiences into which they have entered. How different are the 'activities' of the more respected churches, if they may be judged by the announcements published under that heading—suppers, shows, parties, dances."

While the Church cannot be charged with the full responsibility for the phenomenal growth of the cults, she is not free from blame, and for that reason, if for no other, we should endeavour to help and instruct those who, through lack of teaching or the neglect of Christians have fallen into "the snare of the devil."

The desire "either to tell or to hear some new thing" is not peculiar to the Athenians. From time immemorial there have been those who have a penchant for the bizarre and mysterious, and to such, certain cults, *e.g.* Theosophy and Spiritism, make a special appeal. In a world of suffering both in body and estate, the pursuit of health and prosperity have ever claimed a large and tragic following, as witness the adherents of Christian Science and Unity. As a release from the great emotional stress under which so many live to-day, yet other cults have gained earnest devotees.

A study of the chief of these modern heresies reveals not only a substantial identity with certain of those which distressed the early church, but also a striking, almost monotonous similarity, in their denials of the great essentials of the Christian faith. Very few of them can claim originality in their main tenets. In order that readers may trace for themselves the development of the cults, a very brief synopsis of some of the main heresies of ancient times is given, as well as a brief statement of the doctrines usually held by the orthodox evangelical churches.

Accurate statistics concerning the cults are difficult to arrive at, but if the figures put forward are even "within co-ee" of the truth, they are sufficient to give us serious pause. It would not be difficult to establish the truth of the assertion that many of the cults are gaining adherents at a much faster rate than the churches. This much is certain—the Church has failed to successfully indoctrinate its members so that they are in a position to intelligently meet and combat the pretensions of the heresiarchs.

It is the author's aim in this volume to provide Christian workers with a non-technical and brief but accurate treatment of the origin, history and peculiar doctrinal errors of several of the major cults, supported by documented quotations from their own writings. Copious Scripture references are given throughout in refutation of the errors promulgated by each false system. The attitude adopted is warranted by the statement in Isa. 8 : 20.

"To the law and to the testimony: if they speak not according to this word, it is because there is no light in them,"

and by St. John's test of the spirit of error:

"Believe not every spirit, but try the spirits whether they are of God. . . . Every spirit that confesseth not that Jesus Christ is come in the flesh is not of God."—1 John 4 : 1–3.

If there appears in places to be a touch of acerbity in the treatment, let it be remembered that we are not dealing with personalities, but are endeavouring to expose the subtlety and hatred of a foe who is implacable in his hostility alike to Christ and those who are united to Him by faith. Any Christian who has lost the power to become indignant when the sacredness of our Lord's person and work is desecrated, has drifted a long way from the Master and His apostles. Hear their words in this connection, and imbibe their spirit. Jesus said, "Beware of *false prophets*, which come to you in sheep's clothing, but inwardly they are *ravening wolves*" (Matt. 7 : 15). "Take heed lest any man deceive you : for many shall come in my name, saying, I am Christ, and shall deceive many. . . . For *false Christs* and *false prophets* shall rise, and shall show signs and wonders, to seduce, if it were possible, the very elect" (Mark 13 : 5, 6, 22).

Listen to St. Paul's denunciation of the false teachers : "For I know this, that after my departing, shall *grievous wolves* enter in among you, not sparing the flock" (Acts 20 : 29), "But though we, or an angel from heaven, preach any other gospel unto you than that ye have received, *let him be accursed*. As we said before, so say I now again, If any man preach any other gospel unto you than that ye have received, *let him be accursed*" (Gal. 1 : 8, 9). "I would that they were even *cut off* which trouble you" (Gal. 5 : 12). "There are many unruly and vain talkers and deceivers, specially they of the circumcision : *whose mouths must be stopped*, who subvert whole houses, teaching things which they ought not, for filthy lucre's sake" (Tit. 1 : 10, 11).

St. Peter speaks in similar strain : "There shall be false teachers among you, who privily shall bring in *damnable heresies*, even *denying the Lord* that bought them and bring upon them swift destruction. And many shall follow their pernicious ways, by whom the way of truth shall be evil spoken of . . . whose judgment now of a long time lingereth not, and their damnation slumbereth not" (2 Pet. 2 : 1–3).

Lastly, Jude the brother of our Lord uttered his warning in no uncertain terms : "There are certain men crept in unawares, who were before of old ordained to this condemnation, ungodly men, turning the grace of God into lasciviousness, and *denying the only Lord God* and our Lord Jesus Christ" (Jude 4).

I

ANCIENT HERESIES AND AN ANCIENT CREED

THE Apostle Paul exhorted us to "hold fast the form of sound words in faith and love which are in Christ Jesus," and from ancient times the Apostles' Creed has been of great assistance to the Church in obeying his injunction. Although formulated about the second century, it has held an honoured position throughout succeeding centuries, and is probably still the most widely used of all the confessions of faith. It presents in concise language and in consecutive order the great verities of the Christian faith. Here it is:

I believe
In God the Father Almighty
Maker of heaven and earth:
And in Jesus Christ, His only Son, our Lord,
Who was conceived by the Holy Ghost,
Born of the Virgin Mary,
Suffered under Pontius Pilate,
Was crucified, dead and buried,
He descended into hell;
The third day He rose again from the dead,
He ascended into heaven, and
Sitteth on the right hand of God the Father Almighty;
From thence He shall come to judge the quick and the dead.

I believe
In the Holy Ghost;
The Holy Catholic Church;
The forgiveness of sins;
The Resurrection of the body, and
The life everlasting.   AMEN.

Perhaps it will be helpful to set these truths out in a little more detail. The following statement is substantially the view of evangelical Christians, although there may be divergence on minor points on the part of some.

We believe in the Old and New Testament Scriptures as plenarily inspired of God and wholly trustworthy, and that they are of supreme and final authority in faith and life.

We believe in one God, eternally existing in three persons—Father, Son and Holy Spirit.

We believe that Jesus Christ was begotten of the Holy Spirit, and born of the Virgin Mary, and is true God and true man, inseparably joined in one Person for ever.

We believe that man was created in the image of God, that he sinned and thereby incurred not only physical death, but also spiritual death, which is separation from God; and that all have sinned and come short of the glory of God.

We believe in the personality and malignity of the devil, and the universality and heinousness of sin.

We believe that the Lord Jesus Christ died for our sins according to the Scriptures as a substitutionary sacrifice; and that all who believe in Him are justified on the ground of His shed blood.

We believe that salvation is by grace, through faith, and that all who receive by faith the Lord Jesus Christ are born again of the Holy Spirit and thereby become children of God.

We believe in the physical resurrection of our Lord, in His ascension into heaven, and in His present life there for us, as High Priest and Advocate.

We believe in the personal return of our Lord Jesus Christ.

We believe in the bodily resurrection of the just and the unjust, the everlasting blessedness of the saved, and the everlasting conscious punishment of the finally impenitent.

We believe that the Church is the company of all who have been born again and have been formed by His Spirit into one body of which He is the Head, and the Church is commissioned to go into all the world and preach the gospel to every creature.

With these confessions of faith before us, we shall examine some of the heresies current in the early years of the Christian Church, but before doing so, we should have a clear idea of what the word "heresy" connotes. According to Webster it is, "a doctrine or opinion that is contrary to the fundamental doctrine or creed of any particular church; an error of opinion respecting some fundamental doctrine of religion; an opinion or doctrine tending to create division; an unsound or untenable doctrine of any kind." A heretic is "one whose errors are doctrinal, and usually of a malignant character, tending to subvert the true faith." The word "cult" means simply a "system of religious worship," but has come to be associated largely with systems of religious worship which are heterodox.

It will be observed that in the following heresies, the touch-stone of doctrine is the Person and Work of Christ. This is the rock on which they all split.

The Ebionites or "poor people" were a Judaising sect of the second century, whose error was a denial of the reality of the divine nature of Jesus Christ. They impugned His super-natural birth, maintaining that He was the natural son of Joseph and Mary, but conceded that a divine power descended on Him at His baptism. He was distinguished from other men by a holy life, the endowment of divine gifts, and an un-measured fullness of the Divine Spirit. According to Jerome, they believed in the personal reign of our Lord for a thousand years as the Jewish Messiah. Their fundamental error amounted to a denial of the true deity of Christ.

The Cerinthians were followers of one, Cerinthus, whom tradition stigmatises as the chief antagonist of St. John in Ephesus. Cerinthianism was an offshoot of Ebionism, both having in common the belief that the deity of Christ was based on His baptism and enduement of the Spirit rather than on His supernatural birth. He was distinguished from other men, however, only by His superiority in justice, prudence and wisdom. Their contention was that there was no real and essential union of the two natures of Christ before His baptism. At His baptism the heavenly Christ descended upon Him in the form of a dove, and on the eve of His passion, the Christ again left Jesus, so that Jesus died and rose again, but the Christ, being spiritual, did not suffer.

The Arians, who derived their name from Arius, a presbyter of Alexandria, maintained that our Lord was subordinate to the Father *essentially*, having been created by Him, and not possessing inherent and eternal self-existence. They ascribed pre-existence to Him, but not eternity; divinity but not deity. To them He was a super-angelic creature, through whom all other creatures were made. Their error found its rise in a mis-interpretation of the Scriptures relating to Christ's humiliation, and in mistaking His temporary subordination to the Father for the purpose of His mediatorial work, with an original and permanent inequality.

The Gnostics, against whose teachings St. John contended in his first Epistle, promulgated what has been called the distinctive heresy of the second century. According to Dr. Gwatkin it is "Christianity perverted by learning and speculation." It puts knowledge (*gnosis*) in the place which belongs alone to Christian faith. Professor James Orr describes it as "the fantastic product of the blending of certain Christian ideas, with speculations derived from a medley of sources—philosophies, religions, theosophies, mysteries—jumbled together in an unimaginable welter," and his description of Gnosticism is singularly appropriate to many of the present-day heresies we are about to study. The effect of the findings of the Gnostics was to reduce our Lord's life on earth to an illusion, and to maintain that He was neither born nor did He die. Matter was essentially evil, and the source of all evil. Not only did they discount the true humanity of Christ, but they denied alike the personality of the Supreme God and the free will of man. It is this heresy which accounts for the polemical nature of the first Epistle of St. John.

The Appollinarians, with Appollinarius, Bishop of Laodicea, as their champion, in their laudable eagerness to oppose Arianism in its denial of the deity of Christ, denied the existence of a rational soul in His human nature. His body was merely the case in which the Divine Person of the Son replaced the spiritual part of man. He had merely a body and an animal soul. Since the human soul was regarded as the seat of sin, Christ could not have possessed a human soul. It would necessarily follow that He was not "tempted in all points like as we are," nor was He "made like unto His brethren."

The Nestorians, followers of Nestorius, Bishop of Constantinople, denied the unique personality of Christ by dividing Him into two persons. They contended that the two natures of Christ constituted separate and distinct personalities. In their zeal to correct the error of designating Mary as "Mother of God," without limitation, they fell into the opposite error of dual personality.

The Eutychians embraced the doctrine of Eutyches, Abbot of Constantinople, who, desiring to avoid a duality of persons in Christ, fell into the opposite error of merging the human nature of our Lord into the Divine. He thus denied the integrity of our Lord's two natures, and held the mingling of both into a third nature neither human nor divine.

Such were some of the ancient heresies which confronted the apologists of the Early Church, and they were combated with energy and skill by those who desired to preserve the doctrine of our Lord and His apostles from the encroachments of error. As we face the modern heresies, and discover that all are astray on one or more aspects of the Person and Work of our Lord, we too must meet the challenge by the intelligent use of "the sword of the Spirit which is the Word of God." We have been expressly commanded to "contend earnestly for the faith once for all delivered to saints," and we must be faithful to our trust.

II

ROMAN CATHOLICISM

WE place Roman Catholicism at the head of the list of heresies, since it is the largest and most influential of them all. Its emissaries circle the globe, claiming that their Church alone has universal sovereignty over the souls of men, and having as their avowed objective the bringing of every creature into subjection to the Roman Pontiff.

There is a notion widely current that the Roman Catholic and Protestant Churches are simply different branches of the same Church, each leading, although by different routes, to the same goal. They stand, however, for totally, fundamentally, irreconcilably different religions which lead to goals as far separated as hell is from heaven. Experience has proved that the vast majority of Protestants, if challenged, can give no reasoned basis for their non-adherence to the tenets of the Roman Church, and it is with a view to supplying this lack that we propose to advance seven reasons why no Bible-believing Christian can intelligently be or become a Roman Catholic.

First, let it be understood that we have no desire to speak against Romanists as individuals, for many of them are amiable in disposition and estimable in character. Nor do we doubt that among their priests and nuns, there are men and women who sincerely, though misguidedly, seek to live holy lives. A slight acquaintance with Church history would be sufficient to dispel the idea that there are no true believers within the Roman fold. But these concessions in no way prove that the religious system with which they are united is sanctioned by Scripture or that it enjoys the Divine approval.

Next, let us remember that there is much we hold in common with the Roman Church, which, to its credit, has never wavered in its adherence to the great fundamental doctrines of Holy Writ. With us, she tenaciously holds such doctrines as the plenary inspiration and authority of the Scriptures, the virgin birth and deity of our Lord, His substitutionary death, physical resurrection and ascension, the fact of sin and the certainty of future retribution. In these matters we are more at one with her than with the advanced Modernist.

"If you have so much in common with Rome," it might be objected, "why not, for the sake of unity, concentrate on that which you hold in common, and forget those points on which you differ?"

Why not? If what has been stated above were all, perhaps the difficulty of taking such a course would not be insurmountable. But the truth is that there is scarcely one of these doctrines which Rome has not emasculated or so encrusted with the traditions of her councils, as to almost neutralise them.

REASONS FOR REJECTING ROMAN CATHOLICISM

I. *Because of her attitude to the Scriptures.*

The writer of the Apocalypse gives solemn warning in these words:

"If any man shall add unto these things, God shall add unto him the plagues that are written in this book."—Rev. 22: 18.

How does Rome heed this warning? Pope Pius IV answers for us in his creed. "I most steadfastly admit and embrace apostolic *and ecclesiastical traditions.* . . . I also admit the Holy Scriptures, according to that sense which our holy mother the Church has held . . ." The Council of Trent, while receiving the Scriptures, adds, ". . . and also the traditions relating as well to faith as to morals. . . ." Thus the door is left wide open for the addition to the Word of God of anything the Church may desire.

Hear what the Lord had to say to the Pharisees who adopted the same attitude to Scripture:

"Why do ye also transgress the commandment of God *by your tradition*? Thus have ye made the commandment of God of none effect *by your tradition*."—Matt. 15: 3, 6.

A Roman Catholic may have the Bible, but always plus the traditions of the Church and the interpretations of the Fathers. Pope Pius IV maintained that, "it is manifest by experience, that if the Holy Bible in the vulgar tongue be suffered to be read everywhere without distinction, *more evil than good arises*." In more recent days, however, the Roman Church has given more encouragement to the reading of the Scriptures.

In countries where Romanism is in the saddle, Bible burning is still practised. As recently as 1936 a nun in Canada endeavoured to obtain a Protestant Gospel of John from a Catholic, so that she might burn what she was pleased to call "a pack of lies."

In view of these incontrovertible and documented facts, could we ever unite with a Church which denied us the God-given right of possessing, reading and interpreting for ourselves, under the guidance of the Holy Spirit, the Sacred Scriptures?

II. *Because of her demand of submission to the Pope as an indispensable condition of salvation.*

The attitude of the Roman Catholic to the Papacy, the words of Dr. Hugh Pope, himself a Catholic, make abundantly clear. "For a Catholic, the Papacy is the key to the whole religious question. For, to put it concisely, we believe the doctrines of our faith, not because we fancy we discover them set forth in the New Testament, nor because a vague entity called 'the Church' has held them, but because the visible teaching Church—the Corpus Christi or body of Christ—has taught them, and continues to teach them, through its Head on earth, the Pope, the Successor of St. Peter, the Vicar of Christ."[1]

The claim of Rome that, having a Pontificate of about twenty-five years, from A.D. 42–67, Peter was the first Pope, is without a shred of historical evidence to support it. Luke, the reliable historian, has given us a history of the Church from its founding until thirty years after the resurrection, but there is no record of Peter, the apostle to the circumcision, ever having set foot in Europe. When Paul wrote his Epistle to the Romans in A.D. 58, he sent salutations to twenty-seven Christians there, but Peter was not almong them. Is this omission conceivable if Peter was at that time the Bishop of Rome? In not one of the six epistles he wrote from Rome

[1] *The Papacy*, being Papers from the Summer School of Catholic Studies held at Cambridge, August 7–10, 1923.

does he mention Peter, nor is there any record of Peter having visited Paul while he was in prison—surely an inexcusable neglect of his "beloved brother Paul." Strange, too, that Peter himself wrote no epistles either to or from Rome.

Unam Sanctum, the Bull of Pope Boniface VIII declared by Cardinal Manning to be "Infallible and beyond all doubt an act 'ex cathedra,'" states: "We declare, affirm, define and pronounce it to be necessary to salvation for every human creature to be subject to the Roman Pontiff." In his book,[1] published in 1936, Rev. A. Bonnar contends that this decree is "not a document which the Holy See has in any way retracted." So this preposterous demand of Rome is not out of date.

In support of this view, it is alleged that Pope Pius IX blasphemously asserted, "I alone, despite my unworthiness, am the successor of the apostles, the Vicar of Jesus Christ. . . . I am the way, the truth, and the life." If this be the truth, then submission to him would be most reasonable. But is it the truth?

Even the Roman Catholic Scriptures teach that salvation consists in submission, not to the Pope of Rome, but to the Lord of Glory.

"Neither is there salvation in any other; for there is *none other name* under heaven given among men, whereby we must be saved."—Acts 4: 12.

"No man cometh unto the Father *but by Me*."—John 14: 6.

This being the case, we surely will not entrust our salvation to a fallible Roman priest or Pope, but to our Great High Priest who in heaven still bears in His hands the evidences of our redemption.

III. *Because Romanism teaches a gradation in sin which is foreign to Scripture.*

Sins, Rome teaches, are divided into *mortal*—grievous sins bringing everlasting death, and *venial*—smaller sins, not meriting eternal punishment.

In his book,[2] published with the imprimatur of Cardinal Cullen of Dublin, Furniss writes: "It is a venial sin to steal a little. It is a mortal sin to steal much. . . . If you steal often

[1] *Church and State.*
[2] *What every Christian Should Know and Do.*

a little, when the little sums come to make altogether a large sum, it becomes a mortal sin."

In this way sin is condoned and glossed over by a distinction which is unknown either to Scripture or to reason. Sin is either sin or it is not sin. An ethically perfect God must demand ethical perfection of His creatures, and anything in which we fall short of that perfection is sin, and requires atonement. If venial sins are sins, they need forgiveness. If they are not sins, they need no forgiveness, nor do they require purgatory to expunge them.

The clear, explicit teaching of Scripture is that "the wages of sin"—all sin—"is death" (Rom. 6: 23). We refuse to subscribe to such an immoral doctrine as that set out above.

IV. *Because Romanism denies the privilege of confession direct to Christ, without a priest as intermediary.*

Rome's contention that confession in order to be effective, must be made into the ear of a human priest, is entirely without Scriptural support. Our sins are not forgiven merely because we confess them, else there would be merit in our very confession. They are forgiven because Christ died for them and expiated their guilt.

"If we confess our sins, *He is* faithful and just to forgive us our sins and to cleanse us from all unrighteousness."—1 John 1 : 9.

"I will confess my transgressions unto *the Lord*, and thou forgavest the iniquity of my sin."—Ps. 32 : 5.

"If any man sin, we have an advocate with the Father, Jesus Christ the righteous."—1 John 2 : 2.

Although the publican poured his confession into the ear of no priest, we are assured that "he went down to his house justified" (Luke 18 : 14). The dying thief enjoyed no privileges of priestly mediation, and yet immediately at death, he entered Paradise with his new-found Lord.

Let us not surrender to Rome the blessed, blood-bought right of confessing direct to the One against whom we have sinned, and of receiving absolution at His hand.

The tyranny which the priesthood exercises over the Roman Catholic laity is one of the dark blots on its history. On one occasion Dr. G. F. Pentecost was urged to visit a dying Roman Catholic woman in Boston. She had neglected her religious duties and had fallen out with the priest, who retaliated by refusing to visit her in her dying hour. When Dr. Pentecost came he apprised her of the fact that she had not long to live. She said she knew it, and what could she do? The priest would not come, and even if he did, she was too ill to do any penance. How then could she make her peace with God?

The minister told her that she did not have to make her peace with God, for Christ had already made that peace for her, through the blood of His cross (Col. 1 : 20). He instructed her with such verses as Eph. 2 : 14; Isa. 26 : 3; Rom. 8 : 1, and pointed her to Christ as the One who alone could grant her absolution of her sins. The dying woman turned her face to the wall and was silent for a time. Then she said, "Oh! to think of that! That Christ should have made peace for the likes of me!" But for the timely visit of the messenger of the Cross, this woman would have spent her last moments in fear of purgatory, and would have passed out into the unrelieved darkness of a lost eternity.

V. *Because Romanism admits of many mediators*, whereas the teaching of Scripture is unequivocally clear:

"For there is one God and *one mediator* between God and men, the man Christ Jesus."—1 Tim 2 : 5.

In spite of this clear statement of Scripture, Mary and the saints are interposed between the soul of the Catholic, and Christ. One of the best-known writers on this subject, Liguori,[1] gives us statements of recognised Catholic saints. Here are some of them:

"We often obtain more promptly what we ask by calling on the name of Mary, than by invoking that of Jesus."

"If my Redeemer rejects me on account of my sins and drives me from His sacred feet, I will cast myself at those of His beloved mother, Mary . . . until she has obtained my forgiveness."

"O immaculate Virgin, prevent thy beloved Son, who is irritated by our sins, from abandoning us to the power of the devil."

This is a ghastly travesty of the character of the Christ who loved us enough to give Himself for us. But not content with this, Romanists place the love of Mary on the same level as

[1] *Glories of Mary.*

the love of God! Saint Bonaventure actually says: "Mary so loved the world that she gave her only begotten son." What blasphemous dishonour to God and His Son!

Should a believer in the Deity of Christ tolerate for a moment the intrusion of even a glorified human being between the soul and God? "There is ONE mediator."

VI. *Because Romanism denies the finality of Christ's atoning sacrifice.*

She teaches that the holy eucharist is the real body and blood of Christ, under the outward appearance of the sacrifice of the Cross—a perpetual sacrifice, indispensable to salvation. In the mass, the elements are changed into the veritable body and blood of Christ.

Thus is the simple memorial feast in which we proclaim the Lord's death, till He come, perverted and misconstrued. On no point do the Scriptures speak with greater clarity and emphasis than on the completeness and finality of Christ's atoning sacrifice.

"Nor yet that He should offer Himself *often*, as the High Priest entereth into the holy place every year with blood of others; For then must He often have suffered since the foundation of the world; but now *once* in the end of the world hath He appeared to put away sin by the sacrifice of Himself."—Heb. 9: 25, 26.
"By the which will we are sanctified through the offering of the body of Jesus *once* for all. But this man, after He had once offered one sacrifice for sins for ever, sat down on the right hand of God."—Heb. 10: 10, 12.

With these, and many other passages of Holy Writ to support us, we refute this objectionable and irrational dogma of Rome, and affirm that when Christ cried "It is finished," He was proclaiming a blessed and emancipating truth. His sacrifice was accepted by God, as evidenced in His resurrection from the dead, and needs no repetition.

VII. *Because Romanism, for its own profit, promulgates the unscriptural dogma of purgatory.*

This dogma arises out of the belief that after the pardon of eternal punishment, there still remains a guilt of temporal punishment to be expiated in purgatory, where the soul makes satisfaction for sins committed after baptism, by suffering a longer or shorter time according to the degree of guilt. "All who die at peace with the church but are not perfect, pass into purgatory." "The teaching of the Catholic Church," writes Rev. P. Ryan,[1] "is that there are three states, in the other life—heaven, where those go who die, having no sins upon their souls; hell to which those who die in mortal sin go for ever and ever. . . . There is also a middle state where those go who die having venial sins upon their souls, or who have not expiated the temporal punishment due to their mortal sins."

One would surely expect that for such a terrifying conception, there would be a formidable array of Scripture proofs. But is this the case? In the *Catholic Dictionary*,[2] we read, "We would appeal to those general principles of Scripture, rather than to particular texts often alleged in proof of purgatory. *We doubt if they contain an explicit and direct reference to it.*" (Italics ours).

Is heaven mentioned in Scripture? Many times. And hell? Many times. And purgatory? NOT ONCE. Nor was the idea introduced until the end of the sixth century. It was not decreed as an article of faith of the Roman Church until 1439 at the Council of Florence. Does it not seem strange that the Scriptures are silent concerning it, the early Church knew nothing of it, and fourteen centuries elapsed before even the Roman Church adopted this coffer-filling belief? Do you wonder that Hugh Latimer designated it "Pick-purse Purgatory"?

Protestants do not fully realise that even the devout and faithful, except in rare cases (and even then no one can be sure), must experience the purgatorial fires, "the pains of which are more grievous than all the pains of this world" (Thomas Aquinas).

Even the truly saintly Faber describes it thus:

> "In pain beyond all earthly pains,
> Favourites of Jesus, there they lie,
> Letting the fire burn out their stains
> And worshipping God's purity."

[1] *Catholic Doctrines Explained and Proved.*
[2] *Catholic Dictionary*, 1928, p. 704.

Is this the way Christ treats His favourites? Is this what He meant when He said:

"Come unto Me all ye that labour and are heavy laden, and I will give you rest."—Matt. 11 : 28.

"Let not your heart be troubled. . . . I go to prepare a place for you."—John 14 : 1, 2.

Is purgatory the promised rest, the prepared place? Is this the prospect Paul had in view when he had such a desire to depart and be with Christ, which he maintained was *far better*? (Phil. 1 : 23).

Even a devout Roman Catholic lives in fear of death, but our Lord partook of flesh and blood for the express purpose of delivering them "who through fear of death were all their lifetime subject to bondage" (Heb. 2 : 15). The dogma of purgatory gives the Roman Church the strangle-hold in death as in life. It has led to the iniquitous system of indulgences which is by no means a relic of bygone centuries.

On p. 44 of the booklet, *Spiritual Bouquet offered to souls in Purgatory*, the Saviour is pictured as coming in a vision to St. Gregory, and saying, "My friend, I wish to bestow on you a unique privilege—that is, every soul in purgatory for whom shall be offered thirty masses in your honour, without interruption, shall be delivered immediately, whatsoever be its debt towards me, and moreover, I shall not wait till the masses are said, but shall deliver that soul as soon as the offering is made." Thus, by paying a lump sum, release can be effected.

This religion of superstition and fear, which puts the dead at the mercy of the living is far removed from the teachings of Christ. We have not received "the spirit of bondage again to fear," for "perfect love casts out fear."

With complete confidence in an inspired and infallible Bible, conscious as we are of having deeply sinned, we confess our sin to Christ, our one and only Mediator, and commit our souls to His keeping in the sure and certain confidence that He is faithful to His promise and has cleansed us in the true purgatory, His own blood, "which cleanseth from all sin."

SPIRITISM

ONE baneful effect of war is a recrudescence of Spiritism —the attempt to hold communication with the spirits of the dead through the agency of specially susceptible mediums. When myriads of homes have an empty chair, such a development is easily understood. Lest any in their hour of sorrow and bereavement turn to the wrecker's light of Spiritism instead of to the God of all comfort, we should carefully examine the credentials of this movement.

The revival of Spiritism need not surprise us if we heed the prophecy of St. Paul:

"Now the Spirit speaketh expressly, that in the latter times some shall depart from the faith, giving heed to seducing spirits . . . speaking hypocritically."—1 Tim. 4: 1-2.

It is not without its solemn significance that most spiritists are those who have had some background of spiritual experience. Himself an ex-medium, Rev. W. H. Claggett said, "I have yet to meet the first spiritualist of whom I did not find one of two things to be true—either they were renegade church members who had given up their faith, or they were persons who had at one time been under deep conviction from the Holy Spirit, and had driven away their convictions."[1]

The association of many eminent scientists and literary men with the cult, has given it considerable prestige. But be that as it may, we cannot lightly dismiss the appeal it has made to a section of the community.

THE APPEAL OF SPIRITISM

Curiosity. There are many who delight in dabbling in the mysterious and occult. To such, anything sensational or "spooky" has the attraction of the candle for the moth, and the semi-darkness of the seance affords a welcome field of

[1] *The Mask Torn Off*, p. 5.

experiment. Many, doubtless, are innocent in their approach, but innocence of motive is not necessarily a safeguard. Said Hugh Benson: "To go into seances with good intentions is like holding a smoking concert in a powder magazine, on behalf of an orphan asylum. It is not the least protection to open the concert with prayer: we have no business to be there at all. We are blown up just the same."

Bereavement. The movement has received its greatest impulse from the large number of bereaved who have sought consolation from its teaching. Is their loved one happy? Is he conscious of happenings on earth? Our sympathy goes out to all in such cases. But the tragedy and wrong are when the bereaved one resorts to that which is absolutely forbidden by the Word of God. The Church is blameworthy in this matter in that she has not sounded a clear warning note, nor has she brought the Divine panacea for aching hearts to the great masses of suffering mankind.

Psychic Research. Not a few have embarked upon scientific investigation of the phenomena of Spiritism, only to find that in transgressing the explicit command of God, they have involved themselves in unexpectedly serious consequences.

THE ORIGIN OF SPIRITISM

A reading of ancient history, both sacred and profane, reveals that Spiritism was practised in the very early days of the human race. In the Old Testament, no fewer than nineteen words are used to express its various phases.

One of the earliest of modern spiritists was Andrew Jackson Davis (1826) who, when hypnotised, gave out spirit messages. In 1846 he published some of these under the title *The Principles of Nature, Her Divine Revelations and a Voice to Mankind.*

Its modern revival, however, is attributable to Margaret and Kate Fox, twelve and nine years of age respectively, who in 1848 were the first exponents of table-rappings, etc. Their fame rapidly spread, and Spiritism was re-born. Space forbids any extended reference to them, but suffice it to say that in later life both repudiated the cult of which they had been the unwitting founders, and confessed that the whole thing was the outcome of a hoax. Mr. C. W. Ferguson in his *Confusion of Tongues* informs us that their repudiation is on record in the book *The Deathblow of Spiritism*, by Reuben Briggs Davenport.

The Scripture statement of its origin is clear and explicit. "In the latter days some shall . . . give heed to seducing spirits and doctrines of demons" (1 Tim. 4: 1–2) who are fallen angels in the service of the devil. If ever the devil manifests himself as "an angel of light," it is at the Spiritistic seance.

THE DUPLICITY OF SPIRITISM

Much that passes coin as supernatural in the seance is nothing more than sleight of hand. Lavish use is made of modern discoveries in the producing of fake phenomena. When *The Scientific American* offered $5000 for a proved case of psychic phenomenon, a host of mediums announced their intention of competing for it. But when it was announced that the Chairman of the Committee of Investigation would be Houdini, the greatest master of legerdemain in the world, most of them withdrew! Incidentally the $5000 still remains unclaimed. Houdini himself spent many years in studying and investigating the claims of spiritistic mediums, and dismissed them as utterly unfounded. In his book,[1] Houdini sums up his conclusions in these devastating words: "I have not found one incident that savoured of the genuine. If there had been any real unalloyed demonstrations to work on, one that did not reek of fraud, one that could not be reproduced by earthly powers, then there would be something of a foundation. But up to the present time everything I have investigated has been the result of deluded brains, or those who were too actively willing to believe."

Another magazine, *Science and Invention*, carried a standing offer of $21,000 for any phenomenon that could not be explained, or duplicated by natural or scientific means. This, too, remains unclaimed.

Dr. Felton, former president of Harvard University, once attended a Boston seance, and invoked the spirit of the Greek statesman, Pericles, about whom he had written a learned classic. In due course the spirit of Pericles took possession of the medium. "I put to him a series of questions about Athens of his time," said Dr. Felton, "but he had not only lost all knowledge of all that he had ever done during the forty years of his administration, but he had even forgotten his mother

[1] Houdini, *A Magician Among the Spirits*.

tongue. I could only exclaim with Hamlet: 'Alas, poor ghost,' and turn to my books.''

But while admitting that there is a great deal of chicanery among mediums, we would be going beyond both Scripture and prudence in asserting that Spiritism is all fraudulent. We categorically deny, however, that there is any Scriptural support for the assertion that the spirits of the dead can communicate with the living. From Luke 16: 26 two things are clear: first, that the wicked dead *cannot* communicate with the living; second, that the righteous dead *may not* do so. Those who seek to establish such communication, only succeed in making themselves the prey of evil spirits who feign to be the spirit of the departed dead.

Even when there is absolute honesty on the part of the medium, there is no guarantee that, as Conan Doyle confessed, they may not get into touch with "naughty spirits" which aim to deceive, or that the medium may not be misled by the spirit "control."

A classic illustration of this is cited by Dr. H. A. Ironside. A well-known Los Angeles medium, Helen Templeman, sent him a message purporting to come from Dwight L. Moody, in which the evangelist was supposed to say that he had utterly misunderstood the divine plan when on earth, but was now learning slowly.

"My father was the culprit," the message continued. "He never deviated from the old path, and brought me up that way. But my father was not to blame when I became of age. He was a doer, but had no light on the laws of 'spirit return.' " Unfortunately for the medium and her message, Moody's father died when he was a tiny child! So much for the *bona fides* of the spirit—or of the medium.

But with the evidence before us of such a sane scientist as Sir William Crookes, who testified, "I have talked with the spirit of Katie King scores and scores of times, saw her form appear and disappear, and photographed her forty times with five different cameras," and who declared that every scientific test was applied to eliminate every possibility of fraud, and each experiment was confirmed by other equally prominent scientific men who were present, we cannot lightly say that Spiritism has no basis on fact.

The Results of Spiritism

Christ spoke an eternal truth when He said, "By their fruits ye shall know them." Judged by its fruits, Spiritism has little to offer the seeker. On the contrary, the effects on its devotees have been disastrous.

Physical.—Mediums are frequently overpowered by the controlling spirit, and as in Christ's day, fall down and foam at the mouth. "Their work renders them more and more nervous, more and more excitable, and its only logical sequence is insanity." Sir William Crookes acknowledged that the painful nervous and bodily prostration accompanying the work of the medium, involved a great drain on the vital forces. Is this the effect of true Christianity on its adherents?

Mental.—Still worse are the effects of Spiritism on the minds of its followers. "Tens of thousands of persons are confined in lunatic asylums on account of having tampered with the supernatural," says Dr. Forbes Winslow, the noted alienist. A well-known scientist claims that mediumship has identical pathological symptoms with lunacy. The sphygmograph records absolute similarity between a violent maniac and a spirit medium in the trance state. Dr. A. T. Schofield, the Harley Street brain specialist, stated from a wide experience that professional mediums suffer terribly in body and mind. Another authority states that fifty-eight per cent of all insanity can be traced to the fatally destructive processes of Satanic possession, of which mediumship is the quickest and most direct method. But is not the mark of true spirituality the possession of "a sound mind?"

Moral.—"It is the sublime mission of Spiritism to deliver humanity from the thraldom of matrimony, and to establish sexual emancipation" (Mrs. Woodhull, President of the Spiritist Societies in America). Can a system which permits and encourages such sentiments fail to produce fruit after its kind? Should it find a place within the Christian communion?

Spiritual.—It is here that its most devastating effects are seen. "What is virtue?" asks Dr. Child. "Virtue is good, and sin is good. The woman . . . at Sychar was just as pure in spirit before she met Christ, even though she was a harlot, as she was afterwards when she went to live a different life.

There is no difference between Herod, murderer of babes and Christ the Saviour of men." Can aught but evil result to the spiritual life of medium or sitter from such blatant blasphemy?

Eternal.—Most serious of all, its consequences extend to the world to come. "Sorcerers . . . shall have their part in the lake of fire which is the second death" (Rev. 21: 8). "Without are . . . sorcerers" (Rev. 22: 15). Heaven is closed and hell is open to those who traffic with evil spirits.

Well did Dr. A. T. Pierson utter his warning: "To meddle with this awful realm of spirits, may bring us under the sway of malignant supernatural agents and forces. Not only God, but wicked spirits wield weapons which, to us, are superhuman and supernatural. . . . The devil can sway man by powers which belong to a higher realm; and to dare to invade those forbidden precincts is to venture into an unknown territory, and run corresponding risks, risks which are proportionate to the success of our experiment!"

The Scriptures and Spiritism

One of the greatest of human temptations is to endeavour to lift the veil and penetrate the unseen world, but against this curiosity God's people were solemnly warned. "There shall not be found among you anyone . . . that useth divination . . . or an enchanter, or a witch, or a charmer, or *a consulter with familiar spirits*, or a wizard, or a necromancer. For all that do these things are an abomination unto the Lord" (Deut. 18: 10–12). The passage proceeds to state that it was for this most serious sin and affront to God that the nations of Canaan were to be destroyed.

The practice of Spiritism is roundly condemned and strictly forbidden (Isa. 8: 19, 20). It was to be punished by death (Exod. 22: 18, 19; Lev. 19: 26, 31; 20: 26, 27; Num. 23: 23; Deut. 32: 17; 2 Chron. 33: 6; Ps. 106: 37).

The New Testament is no less vocal than the Old in its warnings. Our Lord cites many instances of foul and unclean spirits dominating men (Mark 1: 23, 24; 9: 25, 26). Two instances are given of possession by more than one demon (Luke 8: 2, 30). The power of spirits to work miracles is acknowledged (Rev. 14: 14). The account is given of the exorcising of a spirit from a medium by the Apostle Paul

(Acts 16: 16–18). The modern rise of Spiritism is one of the predicted signs of the last days, concerning which express warning is given by the Holy Spirit (1 Tim. 4: 1, 2).

The Witch of Endor. One of the foundation passages of the Spiritist position is 1 Sam. 28: 3–25; but rightly interpreted, this incident becomes a liability rather than an asset. The paragraph records the solitary instance in which the spirit of a dead person reappeared on earth. Disregarding the explicit command of God to which he had previously rendered obedience, Saul had resorted to the medium at Endor for comfort, for he was now out of touch with God. He asked for Samuel to be brought up. To the amazement and dismay of both medium and king, God interrupted the seance by causing not an impersonating spirit, but Samuel in person to appear. It is to be noted that the record plainly says, "Samuel said to Saul," thus precluding the possibility of an evil spirit impersonating Samuel. It would seem that God—as He had every right to do—had permitted Samuel to appear to Saul, in order to deliver to him the last terrible message of God's rejection.

In support of this view, one relevant factor was the evident terror and surprise of the medium at the unexpected appearance of Samuel, while another was the exact fulfilment of Samuel's prophecy in the death of Saul. It is clear from the record that Samuel did not appear at the call of the medium, else why should she be so astonished, and cry with a loud voice? God does not permit the spirits of the departed to be at the command of godless mediums on earth. In any case this solitary instance would be slender evidence on which to base the whole superstructure of the Spiritistic system.

It must be recognised that there is not necessarily the uniformity of teaching among the various Spiritist circles which obtains among Christian Scientists. This is recognised by their members. "How can we give the same message when half of us accept reincarnation and the other half hotly deny its possibility; when we have Christian Spiritualists, Jewish Spiritualists, Buddhist Spiritualists and even . . . Atheist Spiritualists."[1]

[1] *Psychic News*, May 15, 1948.

The Heresies of Spiritism

Reasons for rejecting Spiritism:
Its attitude to the Bible.
"To assert that it is a holy and divine book, that God inspired the writers to make known His divine will, is a gross outrage on and misleading to the public."[1]

For answer, see 1 Cor. 2: 9–14; 2 Tim. 3: 16; Heb. 10: 15; 1 Pet. 1: 23–25; 2 Pet. 1: 20, 21.

Its Conception of God

In *The Physical Phenomena in Spiritualism Revealed*, this frank admission of the Spiritist's pantheistic conception of God occurs: "We abrogate the idea of a personal God." The extent to which they are prepared to go in their denunciation of the orthodox conception of God, becomes evident in this quotation.[2]

Question, by Mrs. Connant, medium: "Do you know of any such spirit as a person we call the devil?"

Answer, through the controlling spirit at the seance: "We certainly do, and yet this same devil is our God, our Father."

"The first thing which the orthodox Christian has to face is that the doctrine of the Trinity seems to have no adherents in advanced circles of the spirit world. The divinity of Christ as a co-equal partner with the Father is universally denied. . . . We (i.e. Christians) are taught to believe in the remission of sins to the penitent, through the virtue of Christ's sacrifice and atonement. This doctrine Imperator (i.e. the spirit-control) vigorously combats in a score of passages."[3]

For answer, see Gen. 1: 1; 17: 1; Deut. 6: 4; 33: 27; Ps. 94: 9, 10; 147: 11; Jer. 10: 10; 1 Thess. 1: 9.

Its Dethroning of Christ

"What is the meaning of the word Christ? It is not, as is generally supposed, the Son of the Creator of all things. Any just and perfect being is Christ."

---

[1] *Outlines of Spiritualism*, p. 13.
[2] *The Banner of Light*, November 4, 1865.
[3] Lord Dowding, *Modern Mansions*.

"The miraculous conception of Christ is merely a fabulous tale."[1]

"It is an absurd idea that Jesus was more divine than any other man." "Christ was a medium and reformer in Judea. He now is an advanced spirit in the sixth sphere." "Tom Paine is in the seventh sphere, one above our Lord" (Dr. Weisse, noted spiritist).[2]

For answer, see John 1: 1, 14; Phil. 2: 5–11; Heb. 1: 3, 5, 8; 1 John 2: 22; 4: 1–3; 2 John 7.

Its Rejection of Blood Atonement

"One can see no justice in a vicarious atonement, nor in the God who could be placated by such means."[3]

"Your atonement is the very climax of a deranged imagination, and one that is of the most unrighteous and immoral tendency" (A. J. Davis).

"Advanced spirits do not teach the atonement of Christ" (Nicholas).

For forty years Dr. A. C. Dixon challenged mediums in all parts of the world as to whether they believed in the atoning work of Christ for salvation. In not one case did they do so.

For answer, see Rom. 3: 24; 5: 11; 1 Cor. 11: 23–26; 2 Cor. 5: 14–21; Eph. 1: 7; Col. 1: 20–22; Heb. 9: 26–28; 1 Pet. 2: 24; 3: 18; 1 John 1: 7; 2: 2.

Its Conception of Man

"We reject the conception of fallen creatures. By the fall we understand the descent of spirit into matter."[4]

Its Advocacy of Salvation by Works

"Man is his own saviour" (Rev. W. Stainton Moses).

"In the Spiritualistic hymn-book and prayers the name of Jesus is omitted, and the motto of many is, 'Every man his own saviour' "[5] (Rev. F. Fielding Ould).

For answer, see Rom. 4: 2–5; 5: 1; 6: 23; Eph. 2: 8, 9.

---

[1] *Spiritual Telegraph*, No. 37.
[2] *Demonology or Spiritualism*, p. 147.
[3] A. Conan Doyle, *The New Revelation*, p. 55.
[4] G. G. Andre, *The True Light*, p. 162.
[5] *Light*, July 12, 1919.

Its Denial of a Devil, Evil Spirits and Hell

"Hell, I may say, drops out altogether, as it has long dropped out of the thoughts of every reasonable man."[1]

"There is no devil and no evil spirits." "All spirit people of wisdom know that there is no burning hell, no fearful devil."[2]

"All spirits in the other world are nothing else but the souls of those who have lived here."[3]

The inference from this is, of course, that since there are no angels or evil spirits, communications can be carried on between departed spirits of men and women.

For answers, see Job 1: 6; Jer. 27: 9–10; Zech. 3: 1; Matt. 4: 1; 8: 29; 17: 18; Mark 5: 9–13; Acts 13: 7–12; 16: 16, 18; 1 John 4: 1.

Its Minimising of Sin

"What is evil? Evil does not exist, evil is good. A lie is the truth intrinsically; it holds a lawful place in creation, it is a necessity. What is virtue? Virtue is good, sin is good."

"Vice is sandpaper to the soul." "The degradation of prostitution is a phantom of materialism that belongs to self-righteousness."

"There has been no deed in the catalogue of crime that has not been a valuable experience to the inner being of the man who committed it."[4]

"Never was there any evidence of a fall" (A. Conan Doyle).

For answer, see Matt. 15: 18; John 3: 3; Rom. 6: 23; 7: 5–24; 1 Cor. 2: 14; Gal. 5: 19–21; Col. 2: 13; Heb. 3: 13; 1 John 3: 4.

Its Belittling of the Church

"Spiritualism is vastly more firmly fixed than the rock on which it has been falsely said that Jesus Christ founded His church. . . . If Spiritualism is to live, Christianity must die. They are the antithesis of each other. . . . Modern Spiritualism has come to give it its *coup de grâce*."[5]

For answer, see Rom. 12: 4–8; 1 Cor. 12: 28; Eph. 1: 3–14; 5: 23–27; Col. 1: 18–24; Heb. 13: 17; Jas. 5: 14.

---

[1] A. Conan Doyle, *The New Revelation*, p. 68.
[2] *Outlines of Spiritualism*.
[3] Lanslots, *Spiritualism Unveiled*, p. 36.
[4] Dr. A. B. Childs, *Whatever Is, Is Right*.
[5] Editor of *Mind and Matter*, June 1880.

Its Degrading of Motherhood

"I will exercise that dearest of all rights . . . the right of maternity—in the way which to me seemeth right; and no man, nor set of men, no Church, no State, shall withhold me from the realisation of that purest of all inspirations inherent in every true woman, the right to beget myself when, and by whom, and under such circumstances as to me seem fit and best"[1] (J. M. Spear).

For answer see Deut. 17: 17; Matt. 5: 27, 28; 19: 4–8; Gal. 5: 19; 1 Tim. 3: 2.

We will not pain our readers with more of such blatantly blasphemous quotations. Sufficient are given to demonstrate that Spiritism is inherently and aggressively anti-Christian.

THE TEST OF SPIRITISM

It would be strange indeed if God had left us with no infallible test of the nature of this pseudo-religion. "Believe not every spirit," counsels the aged John, "but test the spirits, whether they be of God" (1 John 4: 1). How can we test them?

Do they speak according to and in harmony with the Word of God? (Isa. 8: 19–20). With the above quotations before us, to ask this question is to answer it.

Do they confess that Jesus Christ is come in the flesh? (1 John 4: 3). If not, they are not of God, but are the spirit of antichrist. In other words, the test is a confession of the full deity and true humanity of Christ. The test question should be addressed, not to the medium, but to the spirit-control. Such was our Lord's method.

Dr. William McAlpine, a medical man, says,[2] "One day, at eight o'clock in the morning, I was called to see a brilliant University girl of twenty-eight. I knew her well. She had a fine appearance. When I arrived her father took me up to her room where she was lying, as white as death, with her hands together. She said: 'Doctor, have you come at last to save me?' I leaned against the bedroom door, and looked at her. Remembering John, first epistle, chapter 4, verses 1–4, I applied the test for the spirits, the confession that Jesus Christ is come in the flesh. She cried out: 'Doctor, they won't let

---

[1] Waggoner, *Modern Spiritualism*, p. 147
[2] *Prophetic News*, October 1935.

me say it!' The demon in possession said, 'Dr. William McAlpine, you kneel before me!' My reply was, 'By the blood of Christ and the victory of Calvary, I command you to come out of her.' At last the girl was delivered, and gloriously converted.''

We think sufficient evidence has been adduced to cause any sincere seeker after truth to shun any connection with Spiritism whatever, whether as participant or observer. To those who may be ensnared by it, God's word is, ''Come out from among them, and be ye separate, and touch not the unclean thing'' (2 Cor. 6: 17).

IV

CHRISTIAN SCIENCE

CHRISTIAN Science is a religious system which majors in a healing ministry. It has attracted many wealthy and cultured people into its ranks, but the majority of its adherents come from the upper middle class. Serenity of life seems to be characteristic of its adherents. Even Mark Twain in his satirical volume[1] concedes: "Personally I have not known a (Christian) Scientist who did not seem serene, contented, unharassed."

There are undoubtedly many substantiated cures as a result of their system of Mind-healing, and this has been responsible for drawing large numbers to a movement which has conferred such real material and physical benefits. There is much in its teaching which is true. It has rightly been said that "a pseudo-science does not necessarily consist wholly of lies. It contains many truths, and even valuable ones. The rottenest bank starts with a little specie. It puts out a thousand promises to pay on the strength of a single dollar, but the dollar is very commonly a good one."

In every city their well-built churches and attractive reading rooms invite the passer-by to enter and read. Although accurate statistics are difficult to obtain, for the church publishes no membership figures, in 1958 there were more than 3,000 congregations scattered throughout the world, and membership might easily be more than 500,000. In 1900 the membership was only 21,040. It would appear that there is not so rapid an increase in membership at the present time. Since Mrs. Eddy's death the organisation has been stabilised and solidified under the control of a Board of Directors. It has been described as "one of the most efficient authoritarian and rigid structures known to religious history."

Great use is made of well-produced literature. The daily newspaper *Christian Science Monitor* maintains a high standard and is widely read. They publish various periodicals and their

[1] Mark Twain, *Christian Science.*

literature is attractively displayed in public places. Somewhat like Roman Catholicism, there is a religious censorship and certain books are not approved for reading. Teachers or practitioners accused of circulating or recommending such are subject to censure or severe discipline.[1] Tremendous pressure is brought to bear upon publishers of books dangerously critical of the movement. A notorious instance was that of the boycott imposed on E. F. Dakin's *Mrs. Eddy, the Biography of a Virginal Mind*, which caused Charles Scribner's Sons to include a brochure in each copy of the book, exposing the methods adopted to keep the book from reaching the public. The author has a copy of this brochure.

This heresy, a recrudescence of the Gnostic heresy of the first century, is a system of healing embodying pantheism and based on the old philosophical concept of the non-existence of matter. Its leading principle is that there is nothing material in the universe; matter does not exist. "Mind is all; matter is naught."

A close examination of the teachings of Christian Science will convince an honest investigator that, in spite of its beneficent features, one could not be at the same time a New Testament Christian and a Christian Scientist.

REASONS FOR NOT EMBRACING CHRISTIAN SCIENCE

Because of its Misleading Name

As has been often stated, it is neither Christian, nor is it Science. The founder, Mrs. Mary Baker Eddy, affirmed, "In 1866 I discovered the science of metaphysical healing, and named it Christian Science." It has been established that she neither discovered it, nor was she the originator of the name.

It is not *Christian*, for it denies or vitiates almost every fundamental truth of Christianity, and indeed, the reality of Christ Himself. Since, according to its founder, there is no such thing as sin, the need of a Saviour is obviated. It is difficult to see on what grounds such a system can style itself Christian. As in many other cults, the device of a double meaning of words is employed. Orthodox terminology is used to convey a heterodox meaning.

It is not *Science*, for it repudiates the findings of science, and substitutes its own contradictory hypotheses. The aid of

[1] C. S. Braden, *Christian Science Today*, p. 124.

medical science is spurned and denounced as positively harmful.

Because of its Heretical Origin

While professing to be very new, it is nothing but a recrudescence of the Gnostic heresy of the first century, as has already been remarked. One of the original editors of Mrs. Eddy's *Science and Health*, Rev. J. H. Wiggin, said, "Christian Science, on its theological side, is an ignorant revival of one form of ancient Gnosticism." It shares the pantheism of Theosophy and Buddhism, while employing much of the terminology of Christianity.

That famous woman, Pandita Ramabai, a high caste Brahmin converted to Christ and the only woman upon whom the honoured title of Pandita had ever been conferred, wrote:

"On my arrival in New York I was told that a new philosophy was being taught in the United States, and that it had won many disciples. The philosophy was called Christian Science, and when I asked what its teaching was, I recognised it as being the same philosophy that has been taught among my people for four thousand years. It has wrecked millions of lives and caused immeasurable suffering and sorrow in my land, for it is based on selfishness and knows no sympathy or compassion. It means just this, the philosophy of nothingness. You are to view the whole universe as nothing but falsehood. You are to think it does not exist. You do not exist. I do not exist. The birds and beasts that you see do not exist. When you realise that you have no personality whatever, then you will have attained the highest perfection of what is called 'Yoga', and that gives you liberation, and you are liberated from your body and you become like him without any personality."

Because of the Dissimulation of its Founder

The character and conduct of its leaders are a legitimate subject of investigation when the nature and claims of a religious movement are under review. The following facts concerning Mrs. Eddy speak for themselves.

Mrs. Eddy's claim to have discovered and named Christian Science in 1866 is contrary to fact. Phineas P. Quimby, from whom she derived very largely her system of mental healing,

gave his system the name "Christian Science" in 1863.[1]
Christian Science apologists have been at great pains to discredit Quimby's influence on Mrs. Eddy and to dissociate
her teachings from his system. Even so recently as 1953
Norman Beasley has followed this line, but the facts and
evidence are all to the contrary. For a full treatment of this
subject the reader is referred to *The Christian Science Myth*,
by Martin and Klann.

Again, she states in her autobiography that she joined the
Tilton Congregational Church at the age of twelve, which age
she chose to parallel the Lord Jesus when He entered the
temple, whereas the clerk of that church declares that she
was seventeen years old, and not twelve. She divorced her
second husband, Dr. Patterson, in 1873 and married Asa G.
Eddy in 1877. She then gave her age as forty, although
actually fifty-six.

While doubtless many benefited physically from them, Mrs.
Eddy's ministrations could hardly be termed altruistic. Her
regular charge for a series of twelve lessons was $300, a large
sum in those days. When she died, her estate amounted to
$3,000,000. On one occasion she said to her literary editor,
"Mr. Wiggin, Christian Science is a good thing. I make ten
thousand a year at it."[2] In 1907 she made a sworn statement
that her taxable property amounted to $19,000, while its
real value was $1,000,000.

In spite of her extravagant claims for the healing powers of
her religion, she herself did not confine herself to purely metaphysical healing.[3] "Because her recourse to dentists, oculists
and physicians was seized upon by her opponents as representing the failure of her teaching, efforts were made—and
are still made—to keep her sufferings and her reliance upon
material aid from public knowledge. But the diaries of her
intimate associates, when they were finally published—particularly that of Calvin Frye, her long-time faithful secretary—
made it all too clear that their beloved founder had many bad
moments in which she sought relief through other means
and methods than straight metaphysical treatment. Confronted with the Frye disclosures long after Mrs. Eddy's

[1] H. W. Dresser, *The Quimby Manuscripts*, p. 388.
[2] Livingstone Wright, *How Rev. Wiggin Rewrote Mrs. Eddy's Book*,
p. 45.
[3] E. F. Dakin, *Mrs. Eddy*, pp. 513-14.

death, the Mother Church Directors admitted that she had taken anaesthetics on occasion for relief from extreme pain, but her teaching permitted this.[1]

Her views on marriage were not such as would inspire confidence in those who believe in the sacredness of the marriage tie. "Marriage is a temporary engagement to be regarded only as long as we believe in mortal mind." In June 1906 she described marriage as "legalised lust."

The present attitude of Christian Science to its Founder was clarified in a statement of the Board of Directors, the ruling body of the church, dated June 5, 1943. This public proclamation, certifying the position of the Mother Church as to Mary Baker Eddy's place in the fulfilment of Bible prophecy, declared: (1) that Mrs. Eddy understood herself to have been singled out by God as the Revelator of Christ to this age, bringing the foretold Comforter; (2) that in giving the full and final revelation of Truth, she regarded herself as the subject of St. John's vision, so that her work was actually "complementary to that of Jesus Christ"; (3) that she was literally the woman of the Apocalypse, exemplifying God's motherhood, while Jesus exemplified God's fatherhood; (4) that she understood herself to be "the God-appointed and God-anointed messenger to this age", being so closely identified with Christian Science, since the revelation and the revelator are inseparable, "that a true sense of her is essential to the understanding of Christian Science"; (5) that it was her very recognition of her status that empowered her to fight off "the dragon", malicious animal magnetism; and (6) that this same recognition of her place and her mission by her followers is vital to the stability and growth of Christian Scientists "today and in succeeding generations."[2]

In *Miscellaneous Documents Relating to Christian Science*, pp. 87 and 111, are reports of Mrs. Eddy having claimed to raise the dead. Norwood reported her having said that if they loved enough, they could raise the dead. "I've done it," she said. Fanny L. Pierce relates that in her Primary Class of 1888 Mrs. Eddy told of having raised the dead and dying, through the realisation of the allness of God.[3] Mrs. Sue Harper Minns states that Mrs. Eddy told the class of

---

[1] C. S. Braden, *Christian Science Today*, p.38.
[2] Ibid., pp. 374-5.
[3] Ibid., p. 368.

1898 of three times having raised the dead. This Mrs. Minns likened to the experience of Jesus who also raised three from the dead.[1] Such claims and their implications require no comment.

Taken together, these facts, altogether apart from her doctrinal deviations, are not calculated to inspire confidence in her claim to divine inspiration and mission.

Because of its Antichristian Doctrine

Dr. A. T. Schofield, the eminent Harley Street physician, after exhaustively investigating this movement, gave as his opinion, "I know, indeed, no other 'religion' which goes to such lengths in denying the fundamentals of our faith as this 'science'. I have not come across any cult that denies that Christ died at all."

That philosophy of life which calls itself Christian Science has been thus summarised by Dr. Radford:

"All is one; the One is Supreme Being, is God. Therefore all is mind. Therefore Mind alone is real, and Matter is not real; we only think it is. Think differently and the disease will disappear. All our ideas of the reality of these things come from something in our nature which is called 'mortal mind,' a sort of perverted intelligence. These wrong ideas we must destroy by simply disbelieving them, and then evil, whether as sin or disease, will disappear and all will be well."

Let us examine some of its tenets, as found in its writings, comparing them with Scripture. Unless otherwise stated, quotations are from the 1913 edition of *Science and Health*.

The Bible

Christian Science is one of a group of heresies which places alongside the Bible another inspired book to which is given equal or even greater authority than the Bible, and which is regarded as its only true and authoritative interpretation. Mrs. Eddy's *Science and Health* is such a book. Of it she wrote: "It was not myself but the divine power of truth and love infinitely above me, which dictated *Science and Health*. I should blush to write this book, as I have, were it of human origin and I apart from God its author; but as I was only a

[1] *We Knew Mary Baker Eddy*, p. 45.

scribe, echoing the harmonies of heaven in divine metaphysics, I cannot be supermodest in my estimation of the Christian Science textbook."[1]

Although thus claimed to be a divine revelation, later editions of *Science and Health* were constantly being altered so that they differed very materially from the earlier ones. She employed Rev. J. H. Wiggin, previously mentioned, a retired Unitarian minister, to edit it, correct its grammar and rearrange its contents. A "thoroughly revised edition" was produced by Mrs. Eddy in 1907, three years before she died, and the text is now standardised.

"The Bible has been my only guide" (p. 20).

"We take the 'inspired word' of the Bible" (p. 493).

"The material record of the Bible is no more important to our well-being than the history of Europe and America."[2]

"Gen. 2: 7. Is this addition to His creation real or unreal? Is it the truth, or is it a lie concerning man and God? It must be a lie, for God presently curses the ground" (p. 45).

"The second chapter of Genesis contains a statement . . . which is the exact opposite of scientific truth" (p. 521, 1906 edition).

"The manifest mistakes in the ancient versions, the thirty thousand different readings in the Old Testament, and the three hundred thousand in the New—these facts show how a material and mortal sense stole into the divine record, darkening to some extent the inspired pages with its own hue."[3]

For answer see Isa. 3: 20; 40: 8; Matt 24: 35; John 10: 35; 17: 17; 2 Tim. 3: 16.

The Trinity

"The theory of three persons in one God (that is a personal Trinity or Tri-unity) suggests heathen gods, rather than the one ever present I AM."[4]

"Belief in the trinity is heathenish" (p. 152).

For answer see Mark 1: 9–11; John 14: 16, 18, 23, 26; Rom. 8: 9–11; 2 Cor. 13: 14.

[1] *Christian Science Journal*, January 1901.
[2] *Miscellaneous Writings*, p. 170.
[3] *Science and Health* (1895), p. 33.
[4] Ibid, p. 152.

God

"Jehovah was a tribal god idolatrously worshipped by Israel, ranking with Baal, Moloch, Vishnu, Aphrodite" (p. 517, 110th edition). And yet in Mark 12: 30, our Lord commands us to love Jehovah with all our hearts. Who is right?

"God is incorporeal, divine, supreme, infinite, mind, soul, principle."[1]

"God is identical with nature" (p. 13).

"God is definitely individual and not personal."[2]

"God is principle, not person" (p. 317, 1910 edition).

For answer see Gen. 1: 1, 26; 14: 22; 17: 1; Deut. 33: 27; Job 31: 14; Isa. 45: 22; 2 Cor. 1: 3; Eph. 2: 12; 1 Pet. 3: 12.

Christ

"Christ is incorporeal, spiritual" (p. 332, 1906 edition).

"Jesus was the offspring of Mary's self-conscious communion with God" (p. 335).

"The virgin mother conceived an idea of God, and gave to her ideal the name of Jesus" (p. 334).

"Jesus made concessions to popular ignorance" (p. 396).

"Jesus is not the Christ."[3]

"Jesus is the human man, and Christ is the divine idea" (p. 473, 1917 edition).

Christian Science makes a distinction between Christ and Jesus. Christ has always existed. Jesus was only a phantom, living in what was only apparently a body. Thus His real humanity is denied. Apply the test of John 1: 14; 1 John 4: 1–3; 2 John 7.

It also denies His deity. "Jesus Christ is not God, as Jesus Himself declared, but the Son of God" (p. 361, 1909 edition).

For answer see Matt. 3: 17; John 1: 1; 12: 33; 19: 33; Rom. 5: 6, 8, 10; 6: 2; 8: 3; 1 Cor. 15: 20; 1 Tim. 3: 16; 1 John 2: 22.

The Holy Spirit

"Christian Science is the Holy Comforter" (p. 227).

---

[1] *Miscellaneous Writings* (1917 edition), p. 465.
[2] *Rudimentary Science*, p. 8.
[3] *Miscellaneous Writings* (1917 edition), p. 84.

"Receiving the Holy Spirit means an enlarged understanding of Christian Science" (p. 351).

"The Holy Spirit is the Science of Christianity" (p. 167). The Christian Scientist thus disposes of the abundant Scripture proof of the personality and deity of the Spirit. He is only "Christian Science".

For answer see Luke 12: 12; John 14: 26; 16: 7–11; Acts 8: 29; 16: 7; Rom. 8: 11.

Man

"Man is not matter; he is not made up of brain, bones and other material elements" (p. 45, 1910 edition).

"There is neither a personal deity, a personal devil, nor a personal man" (p. 146).

"His origin, self-existent and eternal like God" (p. 619).

"Man is neither old nor young; he has neither birth nor death" (p. 140).

"Man originated not from dust."[1]

"Man is, not shall be, perfect and immortal" (p. 426).

For answer see Gen. 1: 27; 1 Cor. 6: 19; 1 Thess. 5: 23.

Sin

"There is no sin" (p. 447, 17th edition).

"Sin exists only in one's belief" (p. 107).

"If the soul could sin or be lost, then God's existence would cease" (p. 111).

"Man is incapable of sin, sickness or death" (p. 475).

"If God or good is real, then evil, the unlikeness of God is unreal."[2]

"Christ came to destroy the belief in sin" (p. 473).

The denial of sin is the basic error of Christian Science. Everything hinges on this. If there is no sin, then there is no accountability to God, no judgment, no need of a Saviour.

For answer, see Gen. 6: 5; Ps. 32: 1; Isa. 1: 18; Ezek. 18: 4; Matt. 1: 21; Rom. 3: 19, 23; 1 John 1: 7, 8, 10; 3: 4; 5: 17.

Atonement

"Jesus bore our infirmities; He knew the error of mortal

---

[1] *Miscellaneous Writings*, p. 57.
[2] *Science and Health* (1910), p. 470.

belief and 'with His stripes (the rejection of mortal error) we are healed' " (p. 20).

"In Science Christ never died."[1]

" Jesus' blood was no more efficacious to cleanse from sin when shed upon the cross, than when it was in His veins" (p. 330).

"Jesus did not suffer on the cross to annul the divine sentence against sin" (p. 328).

"Salvation is not through faith in another's vicarious sacrifice" (p. 327).

"One sacrifice, however great, is insufficient to pay for the debt of sin. The atonement requires constant self-immolation on the sinner's part. That God's wrath should be vented upon His beloved Son is divinely unnatural. Such a theory is man-made. The atonement is a hard problem in theology, but its scientific explanation is that suffering is an error of sinful sense which truth destroys."[2]

For answer, see Exod. 12: 13; Lev. 17: 11; Matt. 26: 27, 28; Col. 1: 20; Heb. 9: 22–26; 1 Pet. 1: 19; 1 John 1: 7; Rev. 1: 5.

Heaven and Hell

"Heaven is not a locality but a state of mind" (p. 187).

"Hell is mortal belief, self-imposed agony" (p. 578).

"Sin exists here or hereafter only so long as the illusion of mortal mind in matter remains. It is a sense of sin, and not a sinful soul that is lost" (p. 311).

For answer see Matt. 8: 12; 10: 28; 25: 46; Luke 16: 23; John 14: 2, 3; 2 Thess. 1: 9; Rev. 14: 10, 11; 20: 12, 15; 21: 8.

Satan and Evil Spirits

"Christian Science teaches that 'the evil one' or one evil, is but another name for the first lie and all liars."[3]

"Devil: A lie, a belief in sin, sickness, death" (p. 584).

"The supposition that there are good and evil spirits is a mistake" (p. 70).

What then did Christ mean in His reference to the betrayer?

---

[1] *Unity of God*, p. 62.
[2] *Science and Health* (1910), p. 23.
[3] Ibid., p. 331.

(John 13 : 27). If there is no Satan, how explain the Book of Revelation? (Rev. 20 : 10).

Resurrection

"Jesus' students, not sufficiently advanced to understand their Master's triumph, did not perform many wonderful works until they saw Him after His crucifixion, and learned that He had not died" (p. 340).

"His disciples believed Jesus to be dead while He was hidden in the sepulchre, whereas He was alive, demonstrating within the narrow tomb the power of the Spirit to overrule mortal sense."[1]

"Jesus restored Lazarus by the understanding that Lazarus had never died, not by an admission that his body had died and then lived again" (p. 45).

Mrs. Stetson, a leading Christian Scientist, claimed on Mrs. Eddy's decease that "the same situation exists today as when Jesus of Nazareth died and was buried. After three days He manifested Himself to prove there is life after death. Mrs. Eddy will do the same, for she occupies in the world today precisely the same position that Jesus did in His day."

For answer, see Mark 16 : 9; Acts 1 : 22; 23 : 8; Rom. 1 : 4; 1 Cor. 15 : 3-4, 20; 1 Pet. 1 : 23; Rev. 1 : 2; 20 : 5.

Prayer

"God is not influenced by man."[2]

"God cannot be moved to do more than He has already done" (pp. 307-8).

"Audible prayer leads to temptation" (p. 312).

"The only beneficial effect is on the mind" (p. 317).

"If prayer nourishes the belief that sin is cancelled, and that man is made better merely by prayer, prayer is an evil" (p. 5).

It would seem that prayer is a logical impossibility to a Christian Scientist. If God is not personal but only principle, then prayer is surely only pious soliloquy or auto-suggestion. The prayer offered in Christian Science gatherings is Mrs. Eddy's version of the Lord's Prayer which runs:

[1] *Miscellaneous Writings*, p. 170.
[2] *Science and Health* (1910), p. 3.

"Our Father-Mother God, all-harmonious, Adorable One, Thy kingdom come; Thou art ever-present. Enable us to know—as in heaven, so on earth—God is omnipotent, supreme. Give us grace for today; feed the famished affections; And love is reflected in love; and God leadeth us not into temptation, but delivereth us from sin, disease and death. For God is infinite, all-power, all life, Truth, Love, over all and All."

For answer, see Matt. 6: 9; John 14: 13; 15: 7; Acts 6: 4; 9: 11; 12: 12; Eph. 6: 18; Phil. 4: 6; Heb. 5: 7; Jas. 5: 16.

Sickness and Death

"Man is never sick" (1906 edition, p. 393).

"Life is real and death is an illusion" (p. 428).

"Sin, sickness and death are states of mortal mind—illusions" (1906 edition, p. 283).

"Man is incapable of death" (1906 edition, p. 475).

"It is mental quackery to make disease a reality, to hold it as something seen and felt—and then to attempt its cure through Mind. It is no less erroneous to believe in the real existence of a tumour, a cancer or decayed lungs, while you argue against their reality, than it is for your patient to feel these ills in physical belief" (p. 395).

Matter

"God is Spirit. Spirit is the opposite of matter. Therefore God never created matter."

"Spirit never created matter."

"Matter is a human concept" (pp. 335, 469).

The foregoing quotations from authorised Christian Science publications are sufficient to establish the fact that this cult denies in effect, if not in word, all the essential doctrines of the Christian faith.

Because of its Unsubstantial Pretensions

That Christian Science has brought healing to many is conceded. That miraculous cures have been wrought is not disputed. But that does not necessarily mean that the God of the Bible is the author of them. Our Lord said, "There shall arise false Christs, and false prophets, and shall show great signs and wonders; insomuch that, if it were possible, they shall deceive the very elect" (Matt. 24: 24). "Many will say, Lord, Lord, have we not . . . in Thy name done many wonderful works? And then I will profess unto them, I never knew you; depart from me ye that work iniquity" (Matt. 7: 22, 23). Obviously not all miracles and wonderful works are an evidence of divine favour, especially if wrought by those who deny the deity of the Son of God.

Many of the cures by Christian Science "are psychosomatic in nature, induced by suggestion and a concentrated form of psycho-therapy which at times has the appearance of a miraculous intervention." "What has been induced by suggestion can be removed by suggestion."[1] The cures of Christian Science are the result not of *divine* healing but of *mental* healing, which has been paralleled in Spiritism and at Lourdes. Healing miracles were not unknown in the ancient Greek temples, nor are they unknown in the Buddhist temples of today.

The evidence goes to prove that most if not all of the cures effected are of the functional and not of the organic type. Mrs. Eddy herself dropped contagious and infectious diseases, surgery and obstetrics from her list. Mr. Alfred Farlow, Chairman of the Publications Committee of the Christian Science Church and President of the Mother Church in Boston, swore under oath that he did not know of any healing ever having been made by Mrs. Eddy of any organic disease in her entire life, except stiff leg.[2] The mind can be a marvellous curative agency, but it has its limits. There is no doubt that many lives have been lost through the inability of Mrs. Eddy and her followers to distinguish between illness caused through germ infection and those stemming from psychological factors.[3]

Senator Works of California gave the U.S.A. Congress an address of an hour and a half during a discussion on hygiene, when he quoted many Christian Science testimonials. The editor of *The Continent* selected eight of the most striking testimonies, and wrote to the eight doctors quoted as having diagnosed the cases as hopeless, receiving replies from seven of these physicians. In each case the physician denied having made such a diagnosis with the alleged conclusion. Such facts speak for themselves and need no elaboration.

[1] W. R. Martin, *Rise of the Cults*, p. 65.
[2] Ibid., pp. 63–4.
[3] Horton, *Christian Deviations*, p. 39.

Let us heed the warning and exhortation given to Timothy: "O Timothy, keep that which is committed to thy trust, avoiding profane and vain babblings, and oppositions of *science, falsely so called*, which some professing, have erred concerning the faith" (1 Tim. 6: 20, 21).

V

UNITY

A MOVEMENT which claims over a million adherents must have attractive features to account for its popularity. Its sponsors showed considerable astuteness in their selection of "The Unity School of Christianity" for the name of the organisation. Amid the welter of rival religious movements, what is more to be desired than unity? And here is a movement which promises it, with health and prosperity as well. But the interested inquirer is given pause when he learns its affinity with such pseudo-religions as Theosophy and Christian Science, although its tenets are distinct from both.

ORIGINATORS

The movement was founded in Kansas City, Missouri, in 1889 by Charles and Myrtle Fillmore, in which year they published the magazine, *Modern Thought*. Fillmore was at the time a cripple, his wife a consumptive and their three children ailing. Through financial reverses, he was unable to provide for his dependents. At this crisis, through listening to a lecture on mental healing, Myrtle Fillmore saw a way out. She reasoned "that there must be a supreme power"— I am quoting from the *Unity Daily Word* of February 1927— "operating upon fixed divine law, and that this law, applied in faith and faithfully, must of necessity set aside all negative or destructive agencies." Her theory worked. The family was cured, and entered upon a new era of prosperity. In 1889 they decided to devote their lives to a propagation of their "discovery". Such was the origin of what has become an organisation with a world-wide reach.

ORGANISATION

The promoters had unusual gifts of organisation, as witness the present-day activities of the movement. Here are some statistics, the latest we have been able to obtain : 7,600 letters are posted daily; 8,400 parcels mailed monthly; 1,000 yearly subscriptions to Unity periodicals daily; 2,000,000 sheets of paper used each month in the printing presses; Silent Unity receives 1,000 requests daily for healing; nearly 1,000,000 magazines monthly. Unity has its own broadcasting station, and correspondence courses are conducted. Their vegetarian café is one of the most beautiful in the world.

One cannot but admire the efficiency and thoroughness with which the tenets of the cult are promulgated.

Origin

A comparison of the teachings of Unity, Christian Science, New Thought and Theosophy will reveal striking similarities, as well as marked differences. C. W. Ferguson asserts that "Unity is undoubtedly joined to the New Thought by an umbilical cord and sired by Christian Science." All four are pantheistic in their philosophy. Christian Science and Unity share a common belief in the non-existence of sin or evil. "Sin, disease and death have no foundation in truth," claims Mrs. Eddy. "There is no sin, sickness and death," asserts Mr. Fillmore. Both lay strong emphasis on mental healing. "God is infinite Mind, Spirit, Soul, Principle," says Mrs. Eddy. "God is Principle, Law, Being, Mind, Spirit," says Mr. Fillmore. Both cults have absent treatment departments for disease. In "Unity" this branch of activity is called Silent Unity. Unlike Christian Science, "Unity" does admit the reality of bodily ills, but contends that we are delivered from sickness by recognising our deity.

Unity and New Thought both emphasise that temporal prosperity inevitably follows prosperous thinking. "Through the power of God in Christ I am saved from the thought of lack, and I am made rich in all my affairs." Like Theosophy, the reincarnation of the soul is one of its tenets, as also is vegetarianism. Their refusal to eat meat has its rise in their belief that the spirits which indwell the animals are beginning a new cycle of life, and are in process of attaining to the highest level of existence—a human being. To kill the animal might adversely affect the onward development of its spirit.

Unity is suspect as a religious movement on two grounds:

(i) *Deception.* We object to the deceptive use of Biblical terms, and of the Scriptures themselves. Orthodox terminology is used, but it is entirely emptied of its original content, and made to mean in many cases the exact opposite of what the Scripture writers clearly taught.

The device of a double vocabulary is characteristic of Unity—using orthodox terms with a heterodox connotation. The normal Christian cursorily reading the following sentence, would be justified in concluding that they were evangelical Christians. "We do most certainly accept the Divinity of Christ and of Jesus Christ, and we believe most thoroughly in the work which he did for mankind."[1] But read later in this chapter the teaching of Unity on the Person and work of Christ and it will be seen that they deny the basic doctrines of evangelical Christianity.

(ii) *Doctrine.* The method of interpretation of "Unity" teachers is fundamentally unsound. It is spiritualising run amok. Here are some glaring examples culled from their writings, as given by C. W. Ferguson:

Jerusalem is not a city; it "signifies the heart centre of the individual consciousness."

Peter was a fisherman and "a fisherman is symbolical of a consciousness that is open to and seeking new ideas."

Samaria signifies "the highest point of the intellectual perception of truth, or the department of objective consciousness that functions through the head."

The parable of Dives and Lazarus is represented as speaking of one man, not of two—a Dr. Jekyll and Mr. Hyde.

Charles Fillmore's "metaphysical interpretation of Psalm 23 is an unwarranted and misleading handling of the Scriptures, and shows Unity up as Christianity without a cross."

"The Lord is my banker; my credit is good. He maketh me to lie down in the consciousness of omnipotent abundance; He giveth me the key to His strongbox. He restoreth my faith in His riches. He guideth me in the paths of prosperity for His name's sake. Yea though I walk through the very shadow of debt, I shall fear no evil for Thou art with me; Thy silver and gold, they secure me. Thou preparest a way for me in the presence of the collector; Thou fillest my wallet with plenty; my measure runneth over. Surely goodness and

---

[1] *Unity*, Vol. 72, No. 2, p. 8.

plenty will follow me all the days of my life; and I shall do business in the name of the Lord for ever."[1]

Then again, in the realm of doctrine, we find most of the fundamental doctrines either neutralised or denied. Compare the statements of "Unity" with the Word of God in reference to the following doctrines:

God

"God is not a being or person having life. . . . God is that invisible, intangible, but very real something that we call life."[2]

"The author of Genesis was evidently a great metaphysician. He being described as God, Lord God and Adam."[3]

"God is the name we give to that unchangeable, inexorable Principle at the source of all existence. . . . He is Principle, impersonal."

"If God were a person. . . ."[4]

Thus God is impersonal.

For answer, see Gen. 1: 1; 11: 7; Deut 4: 35; Matt. 3: 16–17; 28: 19; John 4: 24; 1 Tim. 2: 5.

Christ

"The Bible says that God so loved the world that He gave His only Son, but the Bible does not here refer to Jesus of Nazareth, the outer man; it refers to Christ, the spiritual identity of Jesus, whom He acknowledged in all His ways, and brought forth into His outer, until even the flesh of His body was lifted up, purified, spiritualised, and redeemed. . . . And we are to follow Him, for in each of us is the Christ, the only begotten Son."[5]

"By Christ is not meant the man Jesus."[6] Thus our Lord was a mere man as we are.

For answer, see Isa. 9: 6, 7; John 1: 14, 18; Acts 18: 28; Col. 1: 17; 2: 9; 1 Tim. 3: 16; Heb. 2: 14; 1 John 2: 22.

Holy Spirit

"All is Spirit. The Spirit reigns in all the world." Thus the Holy Spirit too is impersonal.

For answer, see John 14: 26; 15: 26; 16: 8, 13.

---

[1] *Prosperity*, p. 60.
[2] *Lessons in Truth.*
[3] *Christian Healing*, p. 217.
[4] *Lessons in Truth.*
[5] *Unity*, Vol. 57, No. 5, p. 464.
[6] *Unity*, Vol. 48, No. 2, p. 126.

Man

"In his true estate, man is the Christ, the head of the body. The 'I am' or Christ, goes through the body to each centre, quickening, cleansing, purifying the consciousness with the Word of Truth."[1]

"Whatever Jesus of Nazareth did, it is likewise the privilege of every man to do," said Mr. Fillmore. But we have not heard of his raising the dead or calming the storm, or cleansing the leper!

"I am the Son of God."

"I am the only begotten Son, dwelling in the bosom of the Father."

"I am the Christ of God."

"I am the Beloved Son in whom the Father is well-pleased."[2]

The foregoing are statements which followers of the cult are instructed to make with a view to the Realisation of the Son of God.

Thus every man enjoys the same divinity as Christ.

For answer, see Rom. 3: 12; 5: 19–21; 7: 18; 8: 7; 1 Cor. 15: 22; Eph. 2: 8, 9.

Sin

"God is good and God is all, hence there can be no real condition but the good."[3]

"There is no sin, sickness, or death."[4]

"And since God Who sees and understands perfectly, sees no evil because there is no evil, we, when we attain perfect understanding, shall see clearly the unreality and the futility of appearances of evil to which through misunderstanding, men now attribute substance and reality."[5]

"The metaphysician knows that sin, disease and evil have no presence, no being, no reality and no existence in absolute truth."[6]

But even if there were such a thing as sin, how could an impersonal God, such as they believe in, take cognisance of it, and call the sinner to account?

[1] *Unity*, Vol. 48, No. 2, p. 128.
[2] *Christian Healing*, p, 26.
[3] *Christian Healing*.
[4] *What Practical Christianity Stands For*, p. 3.
[5] *Unity*, Vol. 67, No. 1, p. 32.
[6] *Unity Daily Word*.

Thus, since there is no such thing as sin, man is accountable to no one for his actions.

For answer, see Gen. 8: 21; Jer. 17: 9; Matt. 15: 19; John 16: 9; Rom. 3: 23; 14: 23; 2 Tim. 3: 13; 1 Pet. 2: 12, 14; 1 John 1: 8, 10; 3: 4; 5: 17.

The Devil

"There is no personal devil. This is nothing but an adverse state of consciousness which has developed in man and which keeps on prompting him along the lines of the character which he has given it."

"To know yourself as the Son of God is to overcome devil—the personal self."

For answer, see Job 1: 1–3; Matt. 4: 1–11; John 13: 27; Rev. 20: 10.

Atonement

"The atonement is the union of man with God the Father, in Christ. Stating it in terms of mind, we should say that the atonement is the at-one-ment or agreement or reconciliation of man's mind with Divine Mind through the super-consciousness of Christ mind."[1]

"Forgiveness of sin is an erasure of mortal thoughts from consciousness. This brings the inflow of divine love after the mind has been cleansed by the denial of sin."

Thus atonement is no more than the erasure from the mind of a mistaken sense of guilt arising from sin which does not exist. Then why the blood-shedding of the Son of God?

For answer, see Matt. 26: 28; Col. 1: 20; Heb. 9: 22; 10: 11, 14; 1 Pet. 1: 18, 19; 1 John 1: 7.

Resurrection

" Jesus raised his body to the fourth dimension. Every cell of his organism became a purified monad. . . . He has prepared a place for us in the heavens, the omnipresent ether."

"The law of life is based on mind action, and through the mind we resurrect ourselves from the dead."[2]

Thus resurrection of the body by the power of God is denied.

For answer, see John 6: 40; Acts 13: 30, 31; Rom. 8: 11; 1 Cor. 15: 20.

[1] *What Practical Christianity Stands For*, p. 5.
[2] *Christian Healing*.

Sickness

"Unity seems to teach that the body is God and that you cannot be sick, because your body being God cannot be sick. . . . Theologically described, Unity is essentially materialistic pantheism" (a subscriber to *Unity Magazine*, endorsed by the Editor).

"We believe that Jesus Christ, the Son of God, is alive and in the world today. We believe that the 'more abundant life' which Jesus promised, is poured into the race stream as a vitalising energy, and that when accepted by faith, it purifies the life-flow in our bodies and makes us immune to all disease thoughts and disease germ."

And yet many followers of "Unity" are sick and none of them have escaped death.

For answer, see Acts 5: 31; 7: 55; Phil. 2: 9–10; Heb. 2: 9.

Regeneration

"Being 'born again' is not a miraculous change that takes place in a man; it is the establishment in his consciousness of that which has always existed as the main idea in Divine Mind."[1]

Thus man does not require a supernatural and divine Saviour.

For answer, see John 3: 3; 1 Cor. 2: 14; 2 Cor. 5: 17; 1 Pet. 1: 23.

Animals

"We believe that all life is sacred and that man should not kill or be party to killing of animals for food; also that cruelty, war, and wanton destruction of human life will continue so long as men destroy animals."[2]

For answer, see Deut. 14: 4–5; Acts 10: 9–16.

Reincarnation

"We believe the repeated incarnations of man to be a merciful provision of our loving Father to the end that all may have opportunity to attain immortality through regeneration as did Jesus."[3]

---

[1] *Unity Daily Word*, October 1925.
[2] *Statement of Faith*, No. 28.
[3] Unity's *Statement of Faith*, Art. 22.

For answer, see Ps. 16: 10; Acts 13: 35; Heb. 4: 14; 7: 26; 9: 26, 27.

A study of the above quotations from authorised publications of the cult, will convince any unbiased reader that whatever good there may be in some of the teaching, and we do not deny that it has some very attractive aspects, on the whole it is subversive of the truth, and has no real basis for being classed as Christianity at all. The Christ of "Unity" is only the old Gnostic Christ, not the Christ of Paul and of the New Testament.

The main emphasis of "Unity" is on prosperity and health, while the need for salvation, and the vicarious atonement of Christ are ignored.

Dr. Kenneth McKenzie has helpfully written in this connection, "It is a *present-world* cultus. It has no perspective for the future. It deals exclusively with the flesh-life. It demands the best that earth can give and wants it for self-appropriation. . . . When the portals of death open for the entrance of the bewildered soul into the solitude beyond, it has no note of cheer, no hope of immortality."

"Unity" holds out great promises of prosperity, but it has neither ministry nor message to those who have failed. How unlike our Lord, for whom life brought not prosperity but poverty, culminating in a crown of thorns, a scourge and a cross! How contrary to His teaching that His disciples were to deny themselves and take up their cross daily and follow Him! How unlike the teaching of St. Paul which involved him in stripes, imprisonment, distresses!

We would say that the greatest danger in this movement lies in the many beautiful and true sentiments contained in its literature which would appeal to the uninstructed, leading them to believe that they are imbibing true Scripture teaching. Satan does his most dangerous work when he is masquerading as an angel of light.

With an impersonal God, a Christ degraded to the level of man, and man elevated to deity, with a denial of sin and consequent emasculation of the atonement, with self-regeneration and the Hindu doctrine of reincarnation, we are amazed at the temerity of its promoters in designating it a school of "Christianity."

VI

UNITARIANISM

"THE metempsychosis of error and heresy is a very curious thing. When the error or false teaching has been dead for generations, so long that the volumes which entombed it are worm-eaten and the fierce controversies which raged about it are deep in oblivion, lo, the thing comes to life again. The ugly chrysalis of unbelief is transformed into a brilliant butterfly, after which the would-be doubters of the day go in hot and eager pursuit. By-and-by they grow weary in their pursuit, and the butterfly itself loses its vitality as the brilliant colours fade from its wings and it sinks back into the earth whence it came. The new theologies and the new conceptions of Christianity are new only to the age which is beguiled into listening to them and following after them. The history of Christianity shows that in successive generations they have been looked upon as new, whereas they are as old as human unbelief, and that is as ancient as man."

Although written in a different connection, these words are singularly applicable to Unitarianism, which is but a recrudescence of some of the earliest heresies, such as Arianism. As its name suggests, its emphasis is on the Uni-personality of God, in contrast to the Trinitarian view of "One God, eternally existent in three Persons." The name is claimed to be derived from the "Uniti," a society in Transylvania in support of mutual tolerance between Calvinists, Romanists and the Socinians, who were the Unitarians of that day. The name came to be exclusively associated with the associates of the divine Unity, as they were the most active and aggressive members.

A Unitarian, as defined by Webster, is "one who denies the doctrine of the Trinity, and regards the Father as the only God." Such a view necessarily involves its sponsors in a denial of the deity of our Lord. Although given the highest place as man, He is still less than God. In *Leaflet 15 of the British and Foreign Unitarian Association*, it is stated that a

Unitarian is one who believes in the simple unity of God, rejecting the doctrine of the Trinity, and believing in the divine nature of man. In course of time other heterodox features were added, which afforded the movement less and less claim to be regarded as within the pale of Christianity.

On one occasion the great Daniel Webster was dining with a company of literary men in Boston, a Unitarian stronghold, when conversation turned upon Christianity. As the gathering was in honour of Mr. Webster, he was expected to take a leading part in the conversation, and he frankly stated his belief in the Godhood of Christ, and his personal dependence on His atonement. A Unitarian minister opposite him said:

"Mr. Webster, can you comprehend how Jesus Christ could be both God and man?"

Webster fixed his eye on him, and replied:

"No, sir, I cannot comprehend it; and I would be ashamed to acknowledge Him as my Saviour if I could comprehend it. If I could comprehend Him, He could be no greater than myself, and such is my conviction of accountability to God, my sense of sinfulness before Him, and my knowledge of my own incapacity to recover myself, that I feel I need a super-human Saviour." With Webster's reply, all evangelical Christians will find themselves heartily in agreement.

The Rise of Unitarianism

The founder of Unitarianism in its modern form appears to have been Faustus Socinius, who was born of a noble family in Sienna in the sixteenth century. A student of both law and theology, he inherited the papers of his uncle, Laelius Socinius, who adopted a rationalistic approach to the Person of Christ. After living for a considerable period in Florence, Faustus migrated to Poland, where he ended his days. He found there many with Unitarian sympathies, who provided a favourable culture-bed for his doctrines.

Gradually his name became associated with the movement, and the majority of his views, as we shall show, reappear in the Unitarianism of today. His negations of evangelical truth included the denial of the doctrines of the Trinity, the deity of Christ, the personality of the devil, the total depravity of man, the vicarious atonement of Christ, and the eternity of future punishment. Concerning the Person of Christ, the Socinian theory was that Christ, while a divinely commissioned man, had no existence before He was miraculously and sinlessly conceived by the Virgin Mary. Human sin was the imitation of Adam's sin, and human salvation was the imitation and adoption of Christ's virtue. He maintained that the Bible was to be interpreted by human reason, and that its metaphors were not to be taken literally. Satan and the incorrigibly wicked were to be finally annihilated. A review of his teachings reveals the pattern with which we have become so familiar in the preceding studies. In 1660 the Unitarian Church of the Socini in Poland was destroyed by persecution, but in Hungary there were still a hundred churches early in the present century.

THE PROGRESS OF UNITARIANISM

Although the sect fell on evil days on the Continent, it reappeared and thrived in a moderate form in England and America. In England, from 1775 onwards, it enjoyed a period of prosperity, numbering among its advocates such able men as Theophilus Lindsay, Thomas Belsham and James Martineau, who became one of its most influential exponents. In passing, it is worthy of note that after he had reached his eightieth year, Martineau withdrew from the Unitarian church, although he never formally united with any Trinitarian church.

In America, Unitarianism flourished most luxuriantly in New England. As early as 1750, Boston had a group of ministers and laymen who embraced its tenets. The most famous of their advocates was William Ellery Channing (1780–1842), whose blameless character and literary brilliance secured a great audience for his distorted presentation of the fatherhood of God and the brotherhood of man. It must be acknowledged that among their members were a disproportionate number of America's eminent literary men, as Emerson and Holmes, and noted jurists and statesmen, as Adams and Taft.

The growth of the sect resulted in a major cleavage in the Congregational Church of America. Harvard College was captured. Then a large number of cultured and influential people, to whom the Unitarian emphasis on education and practical philanthropy was more palatable than the evangelical advocacy of home and foreign missions, threw in their lot with the popular new religion.

The tragedy of our day is that not all Unitarians are to be found within the communion of that church. All too many fill the pulpits of professedly evangelical churches. It appears to be a matter of policy for a fifth-column of ministers with Unitarian leanings to infiltrate the churches, with a view to future conquest. One minister who himself used to preach Unitarian doctrine, although not formally identified with them, wrote that "although the Unitarians as a denomination are very weak, the spirit of Unitarianism is very prevalent. There are thousands of churches that would resent being classed in such company, but in reality they belong nowhere else. Their evangelism is nothing more than an appeal to the will and their gospel is a setting forth of the manhood of Christ. If it were not for the left-over fire of a former generation they would be as fruitless as the Unitarian denomination itself."

THE DENIALS OF UNITARIANISM

Unitarianism is characterised not so much by its beliefs as by its "unbeliefs," for it is a system of negations. Those truths which we deem fundamental to our faith are ruthlessly rejected.

Dr. Charles W. Eliot, president emeritus of Harvard University, issued a statement of Unitarian belief, portion of which follows:

"We believe in a loving God, who inspires and vivifies the universe, and to that God we attribute in an infinite degree all the finest, noblest, sweetest, loveliest qualities which human nature embodies and displays in infinite forms. . . .

"We Unitarians believe in the essential dignity and goodness of human nature. We believe in goodwill, co-operation for common ends, and freedom from all restraints and subjections, except those involved in preserving the same freedom for thy neighbour.

"We recognise that there are great evils in the world, but refuse to accept them as inevitable, and we combat them with every form of intelligent human effort, and with every means which modern science puts into our hands. . . .

"We recognise that human wills are weak, and human bodies and minds often defective; but we do not infer thence that the human race is depraved and is to be controlled and redeemed only by fear and terror.

"We believe that mankind would get along better than they do now if it were positively known that the heaven of revelation had been burnt and hell quenched."

A perusal of these "beliefs" reveals that they are in essence denials. There is among Unitarians, a marked hostility towards creeds or dogmatic statements, which, they contend, "prison the mind, obstruct the progress of truth, turn attention from plain duties to intellectual and metaphysical subtleties." Herman Randall goes so far as to say, "My own conviction is that if all creeds and dogmas and paraphernalia of the churches in Christendom today could be set aside, nothing would be lost."

We shall now give attention to their teaching.

As to the Trinity

On their own statement quoted above, while holding the unity of God, they reject the doctrine of the Trinity, maintaining that Trinitarians preach three Gods, not one. Actually they cannot claim a monopoly of belief in the Unity of God, for Trinitarians share that view. Their distinctive view is the Uni-personality of God. The *Holy Spirit* is identified with God Himself, being merely the holy influence which the mind of God exerts on the mind of man.

As to Christ

The assertion of the Uni-personality of God necessarily has as its corollary a denial of the deity of Christ, who is reduced to the level of the best of men. How can a system which robs our Lord of His essential deity, possibly expect to be classed as Christian? Actually it classifies itself when brought to the touchstone of Holy Writ.

In his epistles, John makes three categorical statements concerning Jesus of Nazareth.

1. "This is He who came . . . Jesus Christ," or, more accurately, "This is the One COME, even Jesus Christ" (1 John 5: 6).

2. "Jesus Christ is come in the flesh," or "This is Jesus Christ COME *Incarnate*," *i.e.* God Incarnate (1 John 4: 2).

68

3. "Jesus Christ is come in the flesh," or "This is Jesus Christ COMING *Incarnate*" (2 John 7).

In the first, the incarnation is stated historically, in the second, theologically and in the third, eschatologically. Unitarianism is prepared to concede the identity of "the Coming One" with the historic person of Jesus of Nazareth, but denies that He is either God Incarnate COME, or COMING Incarnate again. And in what category do these denials place it? Let St. John himself answer. "Every spirit that confesseth not that this is Jesus Christ COME incarnate, *is not of God, and this is that spirit of antichrist*" (1 John 4 : 2). "For many deceivers are entered into the world, who confess not that this is Jesus Christ COMING Incarnate. *This is a deceiver and an antichrist*" (2 John 7.)

And yet, in spite of the dishonour done to our Lord, they call themselves Christians. In *Unitarian Leaflet No. 13*, their position is clearly stated.

Question 5 : Are Unitarians Christians?

Answer : Yes, but they differ from many, perhaps most Christians, in holding that obedience to the spirit of the teaching of Christ is more important than a correct or uniform intellectual belief with regard to His nature and official position.

Question 6 : How can Unitarians be Christians while denying the divinity of Jesus?

Answer : They deny the *deity* of Jesus but *not* His divinity. Indeed they specially emphasise His divinity as a real and personal quality inherent in His humanity.

Dr. F. S. C. Wicks stated that the dogma he denied was the exclusive divinity of Jesus. He did not believe that the Infinite could be compressed in the form of one being, even so exalted a personality as Jesus.

In Savage's *Unitarian Catechism* the following questions and answers occur :

Question 15 : Did Jesus not say that God was his father?

Answer : Yes ; and he also said that God was the father of all men.

Question 8 : Where was Jesus born?

Answer : Probably in Nazareth. . . .

Question 9 : Why do Matthew and Luke, then, say he was born in Bethlehem?

Answer : These stories about his birth are very late and of

no authority. The Jews expected their Messiah to be born in Bethlehem, so after people came to believe that Jesus was the Messiah, this belief grew up.

Question 61: Did he rise again from the dead?

Answer: There is no reason to suppose that his body lived again.

As to the Scriptures

The supernatural character of the Bible is denied, and its interpretation is on the plane of pure reason. Nothing in the nature of divine inspiration is recognised. Its inspiration is on a level with that of Shakespeare. The existence of God is not a matter of revelation, but a conclusion of reason. Since reason is their supreme guide, the Bible is a source of knowledge only in so far as it coincides with reason. Thus the reason of man and not the Word of the Living God becomes man's final and supreme authority in matters of faith and conduct.

As to the Atonement

The Socinian view of the atonement is still that held by modern Unitarians. Socinius maintained that Christ's death was merely that of a martyr, and that men are inspired to heroic struggle and victory by His unswerving example of loyalty to truth, even though it led to His death. Not God, but only man needs to be reconciled, and since there is no obstacle to pardon in God, no atonement is necessary. Man's sense of sin, guilt and condemnation is purely subjective. All God requires of man is repentance and reformation, which can be effected by man's unaided will.

Such a view of the atonement, while embodying an element of truth, ignores large tracts of Scripture. Jesus was a martyr in the cause of truth, but more, much more than that. All the great and saving elements of the Gospel which have wrought such transformations down the ages, are absent from such an inadequate presentation. In summing up this theory, Dr. E. G. Robinson had this to say, "Unitarianism errs in giving a transforming power to that which works beneficently only after the transformation has been wrought." In other words, it ignores the regenerating work of the Holy Spirit, which alone imparts the power to follow Christ.

As to Total Depravity

The total depravity of man is strenuously denied. On the contrary, "the essential dignity and goodness of human nature" is preached. "We do not infer that the human race is depraved," wrote Eliot.

Unitarians adhere to the Pelagian theory of man's natural innocence and freedom from depraved tendencies—a theory which, of course, comes into violent conflict with the Scriptures. The fall of man, too, is necessarily rejected, and for it is substituted what they are pleased to designate, "the age-long rise of man," whatever that may connote.

Among other heretical views propagated are denial of the sacraments: the purely human character of the Church; repudiation of the final judgment, the resurrection of the body and the everlasting punishment of the finally impenitent. Prayer is robbed of its potency and is explained on a purely rationalistic basis.

DOES UNITARIANISM SATISFY?

But does this belief, or unbelief, satisfy the Unitarian? Let James Martineau, brilliant man of letters answer:

"For myself I own that the literature to which I turn for the nurture and inspiration of faith, hope and love is almost exclusively the product of orthodox versions of the Christian religion. The hymns of Wesley, the prayers of the Friends, the meditations of Law and Tauler, have a quickening and elevating power which I rarely feel in the books on our Unitarian shelves" (*Princeton Review*, 1903, p. 659).

Professor Hale, son of the Dr. Edward Everett Hale, eminent Unitarian preacher who in his old age said, "I do not see why so simple and democratic a religion as Unitarianism has not swept the country long ago," tells of his spiritual pilgrimage in these words:

"The call of Christ I conceive to be that time in a man's life when an impulse comes to surrender everything for Christ. We all come to a place in our lives when we feel that there is something lacking in our life, and Christ speaks to us in that still small voice, and if we accept Him He brings us into the new life. That is what is meant by hearing the call and giving ourselves to Christ.

"Personally I had no expectation that the call of Christ would come to me. I think most who know me personally will agree with me that I was not the man you would have expected to confess Christ. If you will pardon these personal references, I will give a few reasons why. I am of New England birth, and a New Englander is not apt to be carried away by anything emotional. I am a man of books, of an intellectual life, associated constantly with students, and such men do not take such steps under enthusiasm. Most of you are aware of the fact that I was a Unitarian, and that they are known as a sect which lay more stress on reason and intellect than on the heart. Who would have thought that I would have been led to accept Christ in a revival meeting in a Methodist church?

"By my personal experience I can say that the way to the Cross is through prayer. The first sermon preached here by Dr. W. J. Dawson was one on prayer, and it was almost by accident that I happened to go. I only thought of hearing an excellent preacher. I did not find much I had not thought of before; but I said, what he says is sensible, and I will try it; and as I walked down from church that day I prayed that God would give me the best He had for me. Monday came, and I gave myself to the ordinary duties of the week. I did not go to hear Dr. Dawson at once again. It was not until Thursday night that I came; but during that time I continued this express prayer, and I must admit with a little more interest than usual. I went to hear Dr. Dawson again on Friday, Sunday and Monday, and during this time I became conscious of a curious change which was going on in myself, which I did not, and cannot now, explain. Many things which had been much to me—indeed, all—had ceased to interest me. Interest in life began to have a curious dullness in regard to some things. I do not mean in the carrying on of my regular college duties but in art, literature, nature, etc. I began to have a greater love for others, for humanity. . . . On Monday night he preached on the Greeks who came saying, 'We would see Jesus,' and he said that they found, not a philosopher, not a leader, but One whose life had been a sacrifice for the salvation of the world. . . ."

Unitarianism and Modernism

Even a superficial knowledge of the doctrines of Modernism will enable the reader to detect its blood-kinship with Unitarianism, for Modernism is Unitarianism.

The ethics of a minister holding Unitarian views and yet remaining in an evangelical pulpit whence he can disseminate his doctrinal poison, are denounced in no uncertain terms by a Unitarian writer. Referring to a friend of his who each Lord's day recited with his congregation a creed which he no longer believed, he said that he thereby "forfeited his self-respect," and to this verdict we could add that he thereby merited the censure of every true man, and will certainly suffer the judgment of God for preaching "another gospel, which is not another."

One of the outstanding Unitarian-Modernists of Australia was the late Professor S. Angus. A comparison of his creed, given below, with the teachings of Unitarianism will leave the reader in no doubt as to the similarity of the two. And yet for more than twenty years, this man trained the ministers of three of the evangelical denominations. That was surely a major triumph for Unitarianism. Note the significant absences from his statement:

1. We believe in Jesus, the supreme Revealer of God and of man, our only Lord, the Saviour of men.

2. We believe in God, who is Love, over all and in all, the Father of Jesus and of all men.

3. We believe in the Divine Spirit, as the Spirit of God and of the living Lord, dwelling in us, quickening our spiritual natures, making us Christ-like, and so consummating our union with God.

4. We believe in Man, made in the image of God, to show forth his Creator's praise, as by his nature a child of the Heavenly Father; we believe that he can realise his true being only by arising and coming to his Father.

5. We believe that all truth is of God, the ultimate and supreme authority, who reveals His truth by His Spirit in the hearts and consciences of men.

6. We believe in the communion of all those who sincerely love the Lord Jesus, and in that visible form of fellowship—the Church.

7. We believe in such means of grace, sacramental acts, and tokens of fellowship as by experience have proved of spiritual worth to individual believers and to the community of such, especially the books of the Old and New Testaments interpreted in the light of Jesus; the assembling of ourselves together for edification and united worship; prayer as the communion of the soul with God; and the loyal acceptance of an obedience to the will of our Heavenly Father.

8. We believe in Righteousness, Truth, Love, Holiness. Believing in Jesus, we believe that sin can and must be overcome in human life by the grace of God and by the will to choose with which God has endowed our nature.

9. We believe in the ultimate victory of Good over Evil; in God's will being done on earth as in heaven, so that God may be all in all.

10. We believe in Life eternal as the present and ever-increasing knowledge of God through Jesus Christ. In such life there is no death.

This pious-sounding creed is devoid of all the saving features of the Christian gospel, and condemns man to be his own Saviour. The Apostle John had to deal with the Unitarians of his day, of whom Cerinthus was one with a large following. On one occasion when Cerinthus entered the public baths where he was bathing, John immediately left the baths, lest God in judgment strike the place. He wrote an epistle begging true brethren not to receive him or his into their houses. Such was his abhorrence of an error which dethroned his Lord and God. Let us, too, be jealous for His glory, and have no fellowship with those who are following "the spirit of error."

> "Thou art the Everlasting Word,
> The Father's only Son;
> God manifestly seen and heard,
> And heaven's Beloved One;
>   Worthy O Lamb of God art Thou,
>   That every knee to Thee should bow.

> "In thee most perfectly expressed,
> The Father's glories shine,
> Of the full Deity possessed,
> Eternally Divine;
>   Worthy O Lamb of God art Thou,
>   That every knee to Thee should bow."

VII

JEHOVAH'S WITNESSES

ONE of the fastest growing and most aggressive of modern
cults is that known as Jehovah's Witnesses or The
Watchtower Society, with headquarters at 124 Columbia
Heights, New York. Its members evidence an almost fanatical
zeal in the propagation of their views, and in their denunciation of the doctrines of evangelical Christianity. Their operations and literature have spread into 160 countries, and are
still rapidly extending. Since its inception, the movement has
masqueraded under several names, being variously known as
Millennial Dawn, *Metropolitan Pulpit*, *Brooklyn Tabernacle
Pulpit*, *International Bible Students Association*, *The Watchtower Society*, and now *Jehovah's Witnesses*. The latest title
is based on Isaiah 43: 10, "Ye shall be my witnesses, saith
Jehovah."

One cannot but feel that some of these titles have been
ingeniously rather than ingenuously selected. They bear a
close resemblance to some honoured evangelical institution of
the time. Compare International Bible Students Association
with International Bible Reading Association. Compare
Brooklyn Tabernacle Pulpit with that of the great T. de
Witt Talmadge. Compare Metropolitan Pulpit with C. H.
Spurgeon's many publications under that title. This subtle
ruse was obviously adopted to give a semblance of orthodoxy
to a movement which was thoroughly heterodox. Truth has
never found it necessary to adopt the tactics of the chameleon.
That there is a vast and efficient organization behind the
movement is evidenced by the vast coverage of its literature.
As far back as 1952 it was claimed that 22,213,639 copies of
the books of Judge Rutherford were sold, and he claimed
to have sold 130,000,000 copies in ten years. *The Watchtower*
magazine in 1954 had a circulation of 2,000,000 a month in
forty languages, while *Awake*, published in thirteen languages,
had 1,300,000 subscribers. By 1957 the total publication of
magazines had reached the staggering total of 55,000,000

copies in 162 countries in one year. With these figures before us, it is not difficult to believe the claim that the cults publish and distribute more literature than all the Protestant churches combined.

These phenomenal figures are a reflection of the vast amount of time devoted to witnessing by members of the movement. It is claimed that Jehovah's Witnesses devote in each year 34,000,000 man-hours of work in witnessing from door to door and on street corners. Is there nothing for the evangelical churches to learn from the zeal of these misguided people? "People are held and drawn by the very zeal of the movement," says Dr. W. M. Smith. "They are told to distribute periodicals, rap at doors of neighbours, take on missionary activities and promote the teachings of their cult with all the vigour they have. Many people need someone to address them with absolute authority. They need an authoritarian teaching, and such they find in Watchtower literature."

CREDENTIALS

We have every right to demand from this movement its credentials, and considerable light is thrown on its subsequent development by a study of its origins.

Its founder was *Charles Taze Russell*, of Pittsburgh, U.S.A., proprietor of a chain of drapery stores. Finding no existing religion to his liking, he assumed the title "Pastor" and founded one of his own, the most attractive plank of which was the non-existence of hell. As a child he had been haunted by a fear of hell, which resulted from the severe indoctrination received at his church. An atheist whom he met set his mind at rest on this score, and ever after he was the enthusiastic apostle of the doctrine of "no hell". Thenceforth he became increasingly outspoken in his denunciation of organized religion and the clergy.

One would expect that the man who boldly proclaimed the whole church and her ministers to be wrong in their teaching would be meticulously truthful himself. But when under oath in the court at Hamilton, Ontario, he was asked, "Do you know Greek?" He replied, "Oh yes." When handed a Greek New Testament, he proved unable to read the letters of the Greek alphabet. "Now," asked Mr. Staunton, "are you familiar with the Greek language?" Russell unblushingly answered, "No."[1] He then admitted that he knew neither Latin nor Hebrew. Nor had he taken any course in theology. And yet he pronounced all Bible translations unreliable[2] and all other religions anti-Christian.

His domestic relations were anything but happy, ending in divorce, nor was his life free from moral scandal. In the divorce proceedings he received unfavourable publicity in the law-courts. He was ordered to pay £8 per month alimony, but to avoid making payment, he transferred his property worth £60,000 to himself under the name, *The Watchtower Bible and Tract Society*. When, however, this device was discovered, the court later forced him to pay a large sum for arrears of alimony. His financial transactions, especially in the "Miracle Wheat Scandal," brought further dishonour to his name. In court he admitted that there was "some element of truth" in the charge brought by *The Brooklyn Eagle* that he had sold "Miracle Wheat" at $60 a bushel.

Russell's *magnum opus* was his seven-volume *Studies in the Scriptures*, the first of which was published in 1896 and the last in 1917, after his death which occurred in 1916. The posthumous volume caused division within the movement which later resulted in a definite separation. The larger group became known as Jehovah's Witnesses, and the minority group as The Dawn Bible Students. While each of these groups disowns the other, there is a large degree of identity in their teachings. It should be stated that Russell's writings were by no means original. Some years previously, under the title *Day Dawn*, J. H. Paton, of Almond, Michigan, had written his own religious views. The marked similarity between *Day Dawn* and Russell's *Millennial Dawn* leaves only one possible conclusion—appropriation without acknowledgment.

The Test of a Prophet

Deut. 18: 22 says: "When a prophet speaketh in the name of the Lord, if the thing follow not, nor come to pass, that is the thing which the Lord hath not spoken, but the prophet hath spoken it presumptuously; thou shalt not be afraid of him."

"Mr. Russell prophesied that our churches, schools, banks and governments would be completely destroyed by October

[1] J. J. Ross, *Some Facts about the Self-styled Pastor, Charles T. Russell.*
[2] *What Say the Scriptures about Hell ?*, p. 11.

1914. Later, the destruction was promised in instalments ending in 1925. Vol. 4, p. 622 says of the kingdom of God: 'It's influence and work will result in the complete destruction of the "powers that be" of "this present evil world," political, financial, ecclesiastical—by the close of the "times of the Gentiles," October A.D. 1914.' Please observe that in these prophecies the words *complete, final end* and *full establishment* do not admit of any range of option for the events. In an edition of these books showing publisher's date of 1923 the words 'by the close' in the first quotation are changed to 'about the close,' and the words 'by the end' in the second quotation are changed to 'near the end.' Even with these changes the fulfilment is long overdue" (B. H. Shadduck).

Prophecies with Movable Dates

With reference to changes in later editions in the books which have been made to cover failures in the fulfilment of prophecy, Dr. Shadduck writes: "I will not weary the reader with the many prophecies that had movable dates, but I would caution persons having copies of the books that an early publisher's date does not prove that the clumsy revisions that were evidently thrust into a type page already set up were prepared by Mr. Russell before that time. In many cases the revision is so calculated and measured that it fits into a line without disturbing the first and last words of the line, and rarely does it disturb the lines above and below, although there are a very few places where a new paragraph is set in. Vol. 2, with a publisher's date, 1923, shows a chart on p. 247 that dates the destruction of nominal Christendom for 1915. Vol. 7, with a publisher's date five years earlier, has the same chart on p. 595, with the date three years later. Thus it is clear that the earlier publisher's dates may be consorting with the later viewpoint."

Following Russell's death, the reins of leadership passed into the hands of "Judge" J. F. Rutherford, whose title of "Judge" was assumed, for he was never elected to that office. He was born in 1869 and was granted a licence to practise law in 1892. At Columbia, Ohio, in 1931, the name "Jehovah's Witnesses" was adopted by the movement. Dr. Wilbur M. Smith has pointed out that they thus identify themselves with a pre-Christian revelation given to Israel and ignore the New Testament teaching in regard to witnessing. They disown the name "Russellites," reserving it for the "Dawn-ites." They are at pains to deny any theological connection with the discredited Russell, for reasons not difficult to discern. In one of their publications[1] they ask: "Who is preaching the teaching of Pastor Russell? Certainly not Jehovah's Witnesses! They cannot be accused of following him, for they neither quote him as an authority nor publish nor distribute his writings." However, in Judge Rutherford's book *Creation*, written eleven years after Russell's death, we read: "The Lord used Charles T. Russell to write and publish books known as *Studies in the Scriptures* by which the great fundamental truths of the divine plan are clarified. Satan has done his best to destroy these books because they *explain* the Scriptures." In Rutherford's *World Distress*, six pages at the end were devoted to advertising Russell's works. In view of these and many other similar facts, their denial of the substantial identity existing between the teachings of Russell and those of Jehovah's Witnesses is not convincing. Among the Witnesses of today, Russell's writings are little known, and even Rutherford's books are less and less referred to. Only the more recent literature, which is usually anonymous, is considered official and worthy of confidence for this generation.

Since Rutherford's death the flood of literature has not abated. Later publications are often the work of several men rather than of an individual author, but it is justly claimed that these are "just rephrases of Russell's and Rutherford's works, and contain no originality other than up-to-date information on world conditions and new approaches to old material." That there is some divergence in detail is granted, but the major errors of Russell reappear in Rutherford and in the most recent books.

For many years the leadership of the movement has been vested in Nathan H. Knorr, who has been less successful than his two predecessors in gaining personal notoriety. It does not appear, however, that he has been unsuccessful in carrying forward the work with drive and vigour.

With a membership approaching one million around the world, a vast organizational machine has been created characterized by ruthless drive and efficiency. The set-up has been described as follows: "At the head is a central, all-powerful Board of Directors. Under this Board and responsible to it

[1] *Awake*, May 8, 1951, p. 26.

are the various 'Religious Servants' and beneath them the many 'Zone Servants.' The latter have responsibility for the local groups, which are known as 'Companies'. They meet in the 'Kingdom Hall.' At the head of each Company is the 'Service Director,' who is responsible to the Zone Servant for running the Company. He is assisted by a 'service committee' which takes charge of the various activities, particularly of the 'back calls,' that is, repeated visiting of contacts. Women are discouraged from seeking office, and each member of the hierarchy obeys the orders of his superior without question."[1]

They have no salaried ministers, each witness bearing his witness and paying his own expenses. While they have no ordained ministry, a card of identification is given to accredited members who give evidence of being fully devoted to God and His kingdom. They are regarded as unordained ministers and servants of the Lord. They have not hesitated to press this unofficial standing as a ground for exemption from military service.

Considerable astuteness, if not deception, is shown in their attitude to the laws of the State. As their books are only "offered for a donation," not sold, their agents are able to hawk them from door to door without a licence. And since they are gifts, and not articles for sale, they can be sold on Sundays. As "Jehovah's Witnesses" is incorporated as a religious and charitable organization, the sales are not taxable.

Claims

Even if the credentials of its founders be doubtful, it cannot be said that the claims of the movement concerning either its founder or its literature are excessive in their modesty. Russell has this to say concerning his six volumes,[2] *Studies in the Scriptures*: "People cannot see the divine plan by studying the Bible itself. We find also that if anyone lays the Scripture studies aside, even after he has become familiar with them, if he lays them aside and ignores them and goes to the Bible alone, our experience shows that within two years he goes into darkness. On the other hand, if he has merely read the Scripture studies with their references, and has not read a page

[1] Davies, *Christian Deviations*, p. 65.
[2] *Watch Tower*, September 15, 1910.

of the Bible as such, he would be in the light at the end of two years."

On page 348 of his first volume he concludes: "Be it known that no other system of theology ever claims or ever has attempted to harmonize in itself every statement of the Bible, and yet nothing short of this we can claim."

Rutherford is no less bold. In the preface to *Light* he says: "Prior to 1930 there never was a satisfactory explanation of the Revelation published, the manifest reason being that it was not God's due time for his servants to have an understanding thereof." The satisfactory explanation of 1930 was, of course, his own.

CREED

If a movement may be judged by the character and credentials of its founder, then the one under review does not have a very impressive record. But the final test of any movement is the content of its creed. Let us apply this test, giving quotations from their literature and relevant Scriptures. In order that the substantial identity of the teaching of Russell and Rutherford may be seen, quotations are given from the works of both. The books by Rutherford from which we quote are: *Reconciliation, Riches, Prophecy, Let God be True, Harp of God, The Kingdom is at Hand, Creation* and *Deliverance*, while the volume and page of Russell's *Studies in the Scriptures* are also given.

As to the Trinity

Jehovah's Witnesses are unitarian in their teaching on the Godhead. In their writings there is little attempt to understand the Christian doctrine of the Three Persons in the unity of the Godhead. Indeed, in the earlier writings it appeared as though this teaching was deliberately misrepresented and caricatured. It is dismissed as originating among "the ancient Babylonians and Egyptians, and other ancient mythologists."[1]

"There is no authority in the Word of God for the doctrine of the Trinity of the Godhead."[2]

"Nimrod married his mother, Semiramis, so that in a sense

---

[1] *Let God be True*, p. 82.
[2] Vol. 5, pp. 54-60.

he was his own father and his own son. Here was the origin of the trinity doctrine."[1]

"There are some clergymen, no doubt, who are really sincere in thinking that Jesus was his own father, and that the Almighty is the son of himself, and that each of these is a third person, who is the same as the other two, and yet different from them."[2]

"The obvious conclusion is that Satan is the originator of the 'trinity doctrine.'"[3]

For answer, see Isa. 6: 8; Matt. 3: 16, 17; 28: 19; John 1: 1; 1 Cor. 12: 4–6; 2 Cor. 13: 14; 1 John 5: 7, 8.

As to Christ

Christ is regarded only as a created being—the chief of angels, and the highest of God's creation. His true deity is stoutly denied. In support of their doctrine they appeal to their *Emphatic Diaglott* version of the Bible. John 1: 1 is rendered: "In a beginning was the Word, and the Word was with the God, and a god was the Word." Greek scholars combine to pronounce this translation as entirely without warrant, and uphold the rendering in the Authorized Version.

"He was the first and direct creation of Jehovah God. . . . He was the start of God's creative work."[4]

"When Jesus was on earth, He was a perfect man, nothing more and nothing less."[5]

"Jesus was not God the Son."[6]

"Christ Jesus the divine was born three days after the Crucifixion."[7]

"He is a 'mighty God,' but not 'the Almighty God who is Jehovah'" (Isa. 9: 6).[8]

For answer, see Isa. 7: 14; 9: 6; John 1: 1, 14; 5: 18; 8: 58; 10: 30; 14: 9; 17: 5; 20: 31; Acts 17: 31; Rom. 9: 5; Phil. 2: 6–8; Col. 1: 13, 19; 1 Tim. 2: 5; 3: 16; Heb. 1: 8–10; 7: 24; 1 John 5: 20.

[1] Vol. 7, p. 414.
[2] Pennock, *Things the Clergy Never Tells.*
[3] *Let God be True* (1946 edition), p. 82.
[4] *The Kingdom is at Hand*, pp. 46–9.
[5] *Reconciliation*, p. 111.
[6] Ibid., p. 113.
[7] *Deliverance*, p. 245.
[8] *Truth Shall Make You Free*, p. 47.

As to the Holy Spirit

Consistently with their unitarian position, Witnesses deny the personality of the Holy Spirit.

"The Holy Spirit is not a person in the Godhead."[1]

"There is no personal Holy Spirit."[2]

"The Spirit of God is any power or influence which God may be pleased to exercise."[3]

"The Holy Spirit is not a person, and is therefore not one of the gods of the trinity."[4]

In 1,000 pages of Russell's writings there is only one casual reference to the Spirit of God—surely a significant omission. Similarly in the later writings of Jehovah's Witnesses, there is little reference to the Spirit, and whenever the title does occur it is spelt without a capital.

For answer, see John 14: 16–18, 26; 15: 26, 27; 16: 7–14.

As to Man

It is denied that man has a soul. "Man is a soul, but does not have a soul." "The claims of the religionists that man has an immortal soul, and therefore differs from the beast, is not Scriptural."[5]

"Thus it is seen that the serpent (the Devil) is the one who originated the doctrine of the inherent immortality of the soul."[6]

Then why does Paul pray: "I pray God your whole spirit *and soul* and body be preserved blameless"? (1 Thess. 5: 23).

As to the Atonement

The atonement is stripped of any expiatory element, and the idea of substitution is entirely absent. Atonement is conceived to be "the bringing into harmony or 'at-one-ment' with God of so many of His creatures as under full light and knowledge, shall avail themselves of the privileges and opportunities of the New Covenant."

The ransom does not guarantee everlasting life to any man, but only a second chance.[7]

[1] Vol. 5, p. 169.
[2] Vol. 5, p. 210.
[3] *Deliverance*, p. 150; cf. *Let God be True*, p. 89.
[4] *Reconciliation*, p. 115.
[5] *Let God be True*, pp. 59–60.
[6] Ibid, p. 66.
[7] *Let God be True*, pp. 299, 302 (1946 edition).

"That which is redeemed is that which was lost, namely, perfect human life with its rights and earthly prospects."[1]

"One unforfeited life could redeem one forfeited life, but no more. 'Consecrated ones' must carry out their consecration agreement. To turn back would mark them convenant-breakers, worthy of . . . everlasting death." Apparently all Christ's atonement achieved was to purchase for man the right of continued existence.[2]

"As a human being He gave himself as a ransom for men."[3]

"The Lord . . . does not immediately destroy all such ('stubborn, proud, disobedient ones') but gives each one a full and fair opportunity, the Prophet showing that each one shall have at least a hundred years of trial."[4]

Compare these statements with John 10: 30; Rom. 3: 21–26; 5: 1–11; Tit. 3: 5–7; Heb. 9: 22; 10: 12–17; 1 Pet. 1: 18–19; 1 John 2: 2.

As to the Resurrection

Jehovah's Witnesses teach a "spiritual resurrection," whatever that may mean, and deny the physical resurrection of Christ. Using 1 Pet. 3: 8 and 1 Cor. 15: 45, they argue that after His death and resurrection Christ became "a quickening spirit," and "took on different materialized forms." But these verses taken with Rom. 8: 11 teach not that Christ became a spirit being, but that God raised Him through the agency of the Holy Spirit. After His resurrection, Jesus said: "A spirit hath not flesh and bones as ye see me have" (Luke 24: 39), clearly indicating that He was not a spirit, as the Witnesses assert. Did Jesus not claim in John 2: 19–21 that He would raise up the very body the Jews sought to destroy?

"The firstborn one from the dead was not raised out of the grave a human creature but he was raised a spirit."[5]

"So the king Christ Jesus was put to death in the flesh and was resurrected an invisible spirit creature."[6]

"The man Jesus must remain dead for ever if he is to be a substitute for Adam. By that is meant he could not be raised up out of death as a man, and still provide the redemption price for fallen man."[7]

---

[1] *Let God be True*, p. 96.
[2] *Let God be True*, pp. 96, 103, 104, 210, 211 (1946 edition).
[3] Vol. 2, pp. 107–29.
[4] *Harp of God*, p. 336.
[5] *Let God be True*, p. 272.
[6] Ibid. p. 122.
[7] *Reconciliation*, p. 128.

"The Scriptures do not reveal what became of that body."[1]

"We know nothing of what became of it (our Lord's body), except that it did not decay or corrupt. Whether it was dissolved into gases or whether it is preserved somewhere as a grand memorial of God's love . . . no one knows."[2]

"Our Lord's human body . . . was removed from the tomb by the power of God. . . . The Scriptures do not reveal what became of that body, except that it did not decay or corrupt (Acts 2: 27, 31). We can only surmise that the Lord may have preserved it somewhere to exhibit to the people in the Millennial age."[3]

For answer see Mark 16: 14; Luke 24: 39; John 2: 19, 22; 20: 27, 28; Acts 1: 3; 5: 30–32; 7: 55, 56; 1 Cor. 15: 15, 19, 44; Heb. 13: 20; 1 Pet. 1: 3.

As to Sin and Judgment

The Witnesses have evolved a comfortable doctrine which makes a strong appeal to the sinful natural heart. True, the wages of sin is death, but what is death? Annihilation, non-existence. True, the Bible speaks of hell, but what is hell? The tomb, the grave. The large body of Scripture which teaches retribution for sin is ignored or perverted.

"Man by reason of present experience with sin, will be fully forewarned, and when granted a second chance, we may be sure that only a few will receive the penalty, annihilation."[4]

"Man by sin did not lose a heavenly paradise, but only an earthly one."[5] Sin therefore has only a temporal and not an eternal significance, which paves the way for universalism.

"God is too good to sustain an everlasting hell."[6]

"The grave and physical death are the only hell."[7]

"The penalty of the second chance for life will be the second death, which is annihilation."[8]

"The doctrine of eternal torment is as false as its author the devil."[9]

"It is so plain that the Bible hell is the tomb, the grave, that even an honest little child can understand it, but not the religious theologians."[10]

[1] Vol. 1, p. 150.
[2] Vol. 2, p. 129.
[3] Vol. 2, p. 129.
[4] Vol. 1, p. 150.
[5] Vol. 1, p. 177.
[6] Vol. 1, p. 127.
[7] *Reconciliation*, p. 289.
[8] Vol. 1, p. 151.
[9] *Creation*, p. 341.
[10] *Let God be True*, p. 72.

For answer, see Matt. 25: 46; Mark 9: 44–46; Luke 16: 23, 24; John 3: 18, 36; 5: 24, 29; Rom. 6: 23; Rev. 20: 10, 15.

As to Salvation

Since Christ's atoning work on the cross merely guaranteed a second chance, man is left to be his own saviour, and this auto-soterism permeates the literature of the Witnesses.

"Some have been blinded in part, and some completely, by the god of this world, and they must be recovered from blindness as well as from death, that they, each for himself, may have a full chance to prove, by obedience or disobedience, their worthiness of life eternal."[1]

"Men will be given a second chance for salvation during the millennium."[2]

"Second trial will be more favourable than the first."[3]

For answer, see Eph. 2: 8, 9.

As to the Church

According to the Witnesses both Catholic and Protestant ecclesiastical systems had their origin with the devil and are now under his supervision.

"These facts are set forth here, not for the purpose of holding men up to ridicule, but for the purpose of informing the people that the ecclesiastical systems, Catholic and Protestant, are under supervision and control of the devil . . . and therefore constitute the antichrist."[4]

"Organized Christianity is hypocritical and selfish in the extreme. There is no *real* love amongst the people who make up that crowd. The entire crowd is against Jehovah."[5]

"Why do true Christians suffer? Because God has chosen them out of the world and because they refuse to show allegiance unto the Devil's organization."

"The Devil's organization is designated in the prophecies under the symbol of a 'beast,' and also as 'an image of the beast.' "[6]

For answer, see Rev. 5: 9, 10; 7: 9.

[1] Vol. 1, p. 158.
[2] Vol. 5, pp. 17–31.
[3] Vol. 1, p. 143.
[4] *Deliverance*, pp. 222, 226, 230.
[5] *Preparation*, p. 318.
[6] *Deliverance*, pp. 226, 230.

As to Satan

"The ultimate end of Satan is complete annihilation."[1]
For answer, see Rev. 20: 10.

As to the Second Advent

Lurid and sensational interpretations of prophecy are a feature of the movement, nuclear discoveries giving a great boost to their propaganda. Russell claimed that our Lord returned to earth in 1874, and predicted that all saints would be raised in 1914. Later, Jehovah's Witnesses asserted that Christ returned to the Temple in 1914 and cleansed it by 1918, for judgment on sinful men and Satan's organizations. Since Christ did not rise physically, neither did He return physically, nor will He—and this in spite of Acts 1: 11: "This same Jesus shall so come in like manner as ye have seen Him go into heaven." Rev. 1: 7 teaches that "every eye shall see Him."

"In many places in our Bible referring to the second coming of the Lord, the word translated into the English as 'coming' is properly translated 'presence' . . . and refers to the 'invisible presence of the Lord.' "[2]

"We should not expect the Lord's second coming to be in a body visible to human eyes."[3]

As to Earthly Governments

The refusal of the Witnesses to own allegiance to any human government has involved them in a great deal of litigation. They abjure patriotism, considering themselves independent of any government other than Jehovah's theocratic government. They would regard participation in a "theocratic war" a duty, but not in wars between devil-inspired nations.

"Jehovah's Witnesses do not salute the flag of any nation."[4]

"Any national flag is a symbol or image of the sovereign power of that nation."[5]

For answer, see Rom. 13: 1–7.

Other heterodox views held are that the earth is man's heaven and there will be no other.[6] Man has no soul, only body.[7] Christ is not the Mediator for Jehovah's Witnesses, they need none; they are Christ's body.[8] Christ's sacrifice is

---

[1] *Let God be True*, p. 55.
[2] *Harp of God*, p. 225.
[3] Ibid., p. 225.
[4] *Let God be True*, p. 234.
[5] Ibid., p. 235.
[6] *Deliverance*, pp. 335–44.
[7] *Reconciliation*, p. 78.
[8] Ibid., p. 222.

not complete, but is being completed by the Witnesses (His body members) who are being persecuted today.[1] When the Scriptures refer to "that day," they meant 1914, for the world came to an end that year.[2]

Out of their own mouths we have demonstrated that Russell, Rutherford and their followers leave hardly a tenet of the faith intact. Here are some of their errors:

Denial of the Trinity.
Christ was created and not divine until His resurrection.
His was merely a human atonement.
His body was not raised from the dead.
His second advent took place in 1874.
The saints were raised up in 1878.
There is no personal Holy Spirit.
The Lord is now a purely Spirit being.
The Christian Church was rejected of God in 1878.
A second probation for the wicked.
Denial of future punishment.

In view of the above facts and quotations, only a blind credulity or an absolute ignoring of the plain teaching of the Scriptures would permit a Christian believer to embrace this erroneous doctrine. By their repudiation of the doctrine of the Trinity, and their denial of the deity of Christ, they have put themselves outside the pale of the Christian church.

[1] *Reconciliation*, pp. 160, 219.   [2] *Prophecy*, pp. 76, 87.

VIII

THEOSOPHY

THE name adopted by this cult is a happy choice, being as it is, the transliteration of a late Greek word *theosophia*, compounded from "Theo," God and "sophia," wisdom, and which signified "a system of religious teaching claiming an intimate and direct knowledge of God on the part of its privileged initiates." If its name were the true expression of its character and teaching, it would inevitably lead to Christ who is "the wisdom of God." But in fact it leads in the opposite direction.

Great and ambitious claims are made for the movement. It claims to be "nothing less than the bedrock upon which all phases of the world's thought and activity are founded," and "the basic and secret doctrine of all the great religions of antiquity, including Christianity."

In her book *Popular Lectures on Theosophy*, Mrs. Besant wrote: "Occult science (the teachings of Theosophy), takes in the whole of the vast series of changes which begin with the descent of Spirit to embody itself in matter, traces the evolution of forms through stages of ever-increasing beauty, complexity and capacity, so that, within all, the evolving involved life is seen. I have called these stages, these grades, 'The Ladder of Lives.' These living forms occupy successive steps on the ladder, from the mineral to the throne of the LOGOS Himself. It is a veritable Jacob's Ladder, with its foot in the mire of earth and its highest point lost in divine glory."

God, we are told, is to be found not through devout study of the Scriptures, but by looking within ourselves.

"Go then, within, and not without, plunge fearlessly into the depths of your own being; seek in the cavity of your own heart the hidden mystery—the mystery which verily is worthy to be enquired into—and there, there only, you will find Him."

Origin of Theosophy

Unlike many other cults, Theosophy had its birth both outside the white races, and outside the Church. It is a Western adaptation of Hinduism, and was transplanted to Europe by Madame Helena Petrovna Blavatsky. An examination of its strangely mixed tenets reveals that it is a re-hashing of the ancient mystery religions of India, Persia, Egypt, Greece and Rome. To these has been added something of the European philosophies of the Middle Ages and the occult teachings of the Mahatmas, the whole being piously sweetened with the language of Scripture. One writer claims that it is "a mixture of ancient Hinduism, modern Spiritism, Gnosticism and Scriptural phraseology." Referring to its Gnostic tendencies, D. M. Panton asserted that, like Gnosticism, it is a Christian truth disintegrated under a deadly dissolving acid, which distilled by the demonic philosophies of the hoary East, rots away all the heart, while it maintains the husk, of the revelations of God.

Its Hindu origin was frankly owned by Mrs. Annie Besant, Madame Blavatsky's successor, in a *Daily Chronicle* interview. Here are her words: "I confined myself to the Hindu scriptures, and in all cases I stated that I regarded these scriptures and the Hindu religion as the origin of all the scriptures and all religions. This was the position learned from Madame Blavatsky, and which I have held since I joined the Theosophical Society."

The Society was founded in New York in 1875 by Madame Blavatsky, supported by Col. H. S. Olcott and W. Q. Judge. Today it claims to have more than 1,400 branches throughout the world. At the time, the founder said, "It is the same Spiritualism, but under another name!"

The source of Theosophy may be judged from the fact that both of its outstanding leaders were Spiritualists, and that Spiritualistic books are included in the *Catalogue of Theosophical Publications*.

Objectives of Theosophy

These are succinctly stated by Cooper in his *Theosophy Simplified*, p. 1.

1. To form a nucleus of the Universal Brotherhood of Humanity, without distinction of race, creed, sex, caste or colour.

2. To encourage the study of comparative religion, philosophy and science.

3. To investigate the unexplained laws of Nature, and the powers latent in man.

To these objectives as stated, little exception can be taken, except that it throws the door wide open to every creed, or to no creed. But do these three exhaust its objectives and operations? We leave readers to judge. It rather immodestly claims to be the only system which gives a satisfactory solution of such problems as:

The object, use and inhabitation of other planets than the earth.

The geological cataclysms, the differences between the various races of men, the line of future development.

The contrasts and unisons of the world's faiths.

The existence of evil and of sorrow.

The inequalities of society.

The possession by individuals of psychic powers.

ORIGINATORS OF THEOSOPHY

A brief reference to its sponsors is relevant here, and tells its own tale.

Madame Blavatsky, a Russian spiritist medium, was born in 1831. When seventeen she married General Blavatsky, a man of nearly seventy, but deserted him after three months. Since Russian law made no provision for divorce, she "lived a Bohemian life" until she remarried at forty-nine a boy of sixteen who went mad the day after the marriage. Between 1848 and 1857 she claimed to have visited Tibet where she learned the secret of the Mahatmas, of which more later. In 1871 she established a Spiritistic society in Cairo, but encountered trouble for tricking the public. Concerning her, her fellow-worker, Olcott said, "If there ever existed a person in history who was a greater conglomeration of good and bad, light and shadow, wisdom and indiscretion, spiritual insight and lack of commonsense, I cannot recall the name, the circumstances, or the epoch."[1]

In 1884 she was accused of trickery by the Psychical Research Society who had sent a deputation to India to enquire into Theosophy.

[1] *Old Diary Leaves*, Foreword, vii.

Mrs. Annie Besant led "a rather tempestuous life" as a girl. A daughter of the manse, she found it hard to embrace orthodox religion and was constantly assailed by doubts, which were for a time allayed by her marriage to a young clergyman. The marriage, was, however, ill-starred and was later dissolved. She then joined Bradlaugh in his rationalistic crusade, dabbling in Spiritism as a sideline. Incidentally, Mrs. Besant and Bradlaugh were both convicted by the law as publishers of immoral literature, and escaped the penalty only through a legal quibble. When she came into contact with Madame Blavatsky and the Theosophical Society, she found what she had been long seeking, and ultimately became its leader. One of the Societies which she sponsored and introduced to England was "The Order of the Star of the East," whose Declaration of Principles was as follows:

1. We believe that a great Teacher will soon appear in the world, and we wish so to live now that we may be worthy to know Him when He comes.

2. We shall try, therefore, to keep Him in our minds always and to do in His name, and therefore to the best of our ability, all the work which comes to us in our daily occupations.

3. As far as our ordinary duties allow, we shall endeavour to devote a portion of our time each day to some definite work which may help to prepare for His coming.

4. We shall seek to make Devotion, Steadfastness and Gentleness prominent characteristics of our daily life.

5. We shall try to begin and end each day with a short period devoted to the asking of His blessing upon all that we try to do for Him and in His name.

6. We regard it as our special duty to try to recognise and reverence greatness in whomsoever shown, and to strive to co-operate as far as we can with those whom we feel to be spiritually our superiors.

These might be noble aims, were it not that the Great Teacher who has already come is ignored or reduced to the level of Buddha and Confucius. Observe how clever a counterfeit this is of the Scriptural teaching concerning our Lord's Second Advent.

In 1908 she "discovered" Krishnamurti, the coming World Teacher, the Messiah, who, alas, sadly disappointed her hopes.

OBJECTIONS TO THEOSOPHY

Theosophy does not concede the pre-eminence of Christianity over all other religions. Rather does it reduce it to the level of the other religions of the world.

"Theosophy comes to the world then as a peacemaker. Why should we quarrel? God is the Centre, and from any point of the circumference you can direct your steps towards Him; yet in stepping, each will take a different direction towards the Centre, according to the point from which he starts. So it is with all the various religions; they are all ways to God."[1] Mrs. Besant contends that each religion has a note of its own which it contributes to the world. When blended together they give the whiteness of truth, and a mighty chord of perfection. Such a contention is refuted by Gal. 1: 8; 2 John 10: 11.

God

The character of any religious system can be tested by its relation to the great central facts of Christianity. Let us apply this test to Theosophy. What does it teach concerning God.

"The next matter impressed on the student of Theosophy is the denial of a personal God."

"In Theology, Theosophy is pantheistic—God is all, and all is God."[2]

In the *Key to Theosophy*, Madame Blavatsky is asked, "Do you believe in God, the God of a Christian?" The answer is: "In such a God we do not believe; we reject the idea of a personal extra-cosmic and anthropomorphic God, who is but the gigantic shadow of a man, and not of man at his best— this God is a bundle of contradictions and a logical impossibility." To one who protested that if her pantheistic idea of God were true, God would be in the ash of a cigar, just as in the soul of a man, she replied, "To be sure, God is in the ash just as in my soul."

"We do not at all deny the charge of atheism, the word being used in the ordinary theistic sense."[3]

Theosophy has a trinity, but it is only "a threefold manifestation of Power or Will, Wisdom and Activity."

[1] *Popular Lectures on Theosophy.*
[2] Besant, *Exposition of Theosophy*, p. 28.
[3] *The Theosophist*, September 1882.

The trinity of the Theosophist consists of:

The great unknowable, unknown God, corresponding to the Father.

The unmanifested God—the great primeval cause of all.

The manifested Logos.

To these may be added "a Fourth Person, or in some religions called a second trinity, feminine, the Mother."

For answer see Gen. 17: 1; Ps. 103: 13; Eph. 1: 9, 11; 1 Thess. 1: 9; 1 Tim. 6: 16; Heb. 11: 6.

Christ

"This word 'the Christ' means to us more than the name of one, however lofty or however holy, and to us the Christ is less an external Saviour, than a living Presence in the human spirit, a presence by which the human spirit unfolds its innate divinity, so that in time all men become Christs."

"He is the Master to whom the Christian should turn. But . . . there are other Divine Teachers in other faiths, and they occupy to the millions of souls who worship them the same position of Divine-human teachers as the great Master, Jesus, holds in the Christian Church."[1]

Mrs. Besant affirms that Christ was born in 105 B.C.; that He entered a monastery and there met learned visitors from India and Egypt who initiated Him into the Eastern mysteries. The "Christ part" of His nature received at baptism, left His body after the crucifixion (cf. 1 John 2: 22). He later returned in a spiritual body and for fifty years initiated His disciples into the mysteries He had learned.

Thus Theosophy treats with disdain the facts of history, and aligns the Son of God with Osiris, Zoroaster and Krishna.

For answer, see Isa. 9: 6; John 1: 1, 14; 17: 5; Col. 1: 17; 2: 9; Heb. 2: 14.

Man

Theosophy has discovered that man consists of one spirit, Atma. Three souls, Buddahi, Manas and Kamarupha. A life principle, Prana. Two bodies, the astral and physical. The Atma is the reincarnating ego, which is the permanent individuality. Man's spirit is pre-existent. He must work out his own salvation, through many incarnations.

[1] Besant, *Is Theosophy Antichristian?*, pp. 16, 21.

"He, man, is not born, nor doth he die, nor having been, ceaseth he any more to be."[1]

For answer, see Rom. 3: 12; 5: 19-21; I Cor. 15: 22; Eph. 2: 8-9; Tit. 3: 5.

The Bible

"I confined myself to the Hindu Scriptures, and in all cases I stated that I regarded these Scriptures and the Hindu religion as the origin of all the Scriptures and all the religions."[2] (Annie Besant.)

Theosophists interpret the Bible, not in order to find authority for their own teaching, but to find spiritual significance for the comfort of Christians who have outgrown the plain meaning of the Bible and yet are unwilling to abandon a book which has such sacred and familiar associations. The appointed mission of Theosophy is "the unsealing of the Bibles of the West" with an Eastern Key.[3]

"The Bible is only one of many revelations."

But to the Christian who accepts the authority of the Scriptures, God has spoken His final word in Christ. We will look in vain for any new revelation than that which is already given in the Bible.

For answer, see Isa. 8: 19, 20; Matt. 4: 1-11; 5: 18; John 12: 48; 2 Tim. 3: 16; Heb. 4: 12; Rev. 22: 18, 19.

Sin

"The Fall of man does not mean, as commonly supposed, the lapse, through a specific act, of particular individuals from a state of original perfection."[4] On being asked if lying, adultery, and murder were not wrong in themselves, Subramannya Ayah, a leading Theosophist replied, "No, these things are only wrong if a man thinks them wrong; but if he thinks them right, it is right for him to do them."

Thus Theosophy refuses to acknowledge the most elementary moral standards.

For answer, see Gen. 3: 6, 7; Rom. 5: 12.

---

[1] Cooper, *Theosophy Simplified*, p. 30.
[2] *The Daily Chronicle*, April 9, 1894.
[3] Radford, *Ancient Heresies in Modern Dress*, p. 303.
[4] *The Perfect Way*, p. 215.

Vicarious Atonement

"The atonement wrought by Christ lies not in the substitution of one individual for another, but in the identity of nature between the divine man, and men who are becoming divine."[1]

"We believe neither in vicarious atonement, nor in the possibility of the remission of the smallest sin by any god, not even by a personal Absolute or Infinite, if such a thing could have existence."[2]

For answer, see Matt. 20: 28; 26: 28; John 4: 51–55; 10: 11; 2 Cor. 5: 21; Gal. 3: 10, 13; 1 Tim. 2: 6; 1 Pet. 2: 24.

The Devil

"There is no personal devil. That which mystically is called the Devil, is the negation and opposite of God. And whereas God is I AM or positive Being, the Devil is NOT."

"The Devil is not to be confounded with 'Satan,' though they are sometimes spoken of in Scripture as if they were identical. In such cases, however, Scripture presents but the popular belief."[3]

For answer, see Matt. 4: 1–4; Rev. 20: 2, 10.

Prayer

"Whether the person pray to Buddha, to Vishnu, to Christ, to the Father, it matters not at all."[4]

For answer, see John 14: 13, 14; 15: 7; 16: 24; Heb. 11: 6.

Hell

"If this (Luke 13: 23, 24) be applied in the ordinary Protestant way to salvation, from everlasting hell-fire, the statement becomes incredible, shocking."[5]

For answer, see Matt. 25: 41, 46; John 3: 36; 2 Thess. 1: 9; Rev. 20: 14, 15.

Such are Theosophy's direct denials of the faith. But in addition, there are certain Buddhist accretions which do violence alike to Scripture and to common sense. Chief among these are the teachings concerning:

---

[1] *Is Theosophy Antichristian?*, p. 15.
[2] *Key of Theosophy*, p. 135.
[3] *The Perfect Way*, pp. 69–71.
[4] Besant, *The Seven Principles of Man*, p. 58.
[5] Besant, *Esoteric Christianity*, p. 42.

REINCARNATION

Theosophy's basic belief is the doctrine of the evolution of the soul by repeated incarnations. The idea behind this doctrine is that, if each action produces eternal results, then there must be some existence in which these results manifest themselves. As we admittedly do not experience the results of all our actions in this life, there must be other lives in which those results come forth. Each action in this life issues in an experience in the life to come. There may be a transmigration of soul to the form of a plant, or a lower animal, or a human being, according to the merit or demerit of the past life. When Mrs. Besant first met Bradlaugh, she said: "I know that our instinctive friendliness was in very truth an outgrowth of friendship in other lives, and that on that August day we took up again that ancient tie, and did not begin a new one."[1]

"Reincarnation is taken for granted in the whole of this teaching."

The New Schaff-Herzog Religious Encyclopaedia summarises the Theosophical teaching on reincarnation:

"The unfoldment of man's powers is slow and gradual; hence the necessity of repeated incarnations, each life on earth being like a day in school. At death a man drops his physical body, and clothed in his subtle bodies, lives a life of purification, rest and bliss, rich and full in proportion to his stage in evolution and the needs of the life just ended. This is the time when he assimilates the experiences of that life, changing them into faculties. As this work is being done, he drops one after the other his worn-out astral bodies, and finally, having enjoyed all the bliss to which his achievements entitle him, he clothes himself in new bodies and returns to earth to take up the earth existence where he had left it, each life being thus a progress on the preceding one."

For such a doctrine they produce not one scintilla of evidence. Mrs. Besant herself admits that "the only proof of the doctrine must in the nature of things lie in the future, if it exists at all."[2]

For answer see Heb. 9: 26, 27.

[1] *An Autobiography*, p. 136.
[2] *Why I Became a Theosophist.*

KARMA, THE LAW OF RETRIBUTION

In place of the soul-satisfying Christian doctrine of forgiveness of sins through the atonement of Christ, the Theosophist is offered the myth of reincarnation, which has a twin-principle in the Buddhist idea of "Karma." The Theosophist is always trying to "make good Karma"—i.e. to add to his store of merit. Karma is defined as "action, deed, effect, fate." It is the law of sowing and reaping. If you do not wish to reap, then do not sow. If you wish to avoid an effect, refrain from doing that which would cause that effect. What a man reaps in his present life, he has sown in some previous existence. In his book on India (p. 364) J. P. Jones defines the word as meaning, "actions pursuing the soul through successive births, and compelling it to reveal by its conditions and reflect by its experiences the previous birth." But as Van Baalen points out, all suffering is not the outcome of evil deeds, nor is there anything ethical, or purging in suffering for evil deeds of which one has no memory. Indeed, much of our suffering comes through the evil deeds of others.

For answer, see Isa. 1: 18; 1 John 1: 9.

THE MAHATMAS

Madame Blavatsky claimed to have penetrated Tibet, and there to have held communion with the Mahatmas, or Brotherhood of Teachers, men of superior wisdom, "the finished product of human evolution," as far above ordinary mankind as man is above the insects of the fields. According to Mrs. Besant, a Mahatma is "a living man who has evolved more rapidly than the vast majority of the human race, and has reached a stage of mental, moral and spiritual development which will be attained by the race in the future only at the end of millenniums of years."[1]

The great objective of the Theosophist is, by the purging of successive incarnations, to become an initiate, and be welcomed by this great Brotherhood of Teachers. These Mahatmas are the source of the knowledge of occult matters claimed by Theosophy.[2]

"If there are no Masters," asserted Mrs. Besant, "then the Theosophical Society is an absurdity." Supreme over the

[1] *Exposition of Theosophy*, p. 19.
[2] *Lucifer*, December 15, 1890.

Mahatmas is the Great World Teacher who will, when he finds a suitable medium, give to the world a greater and higher revelation.

For answer, see Matt. 24: 24–26.

KRISHNAMURTI

Theosophy thoroughly discredited itself and irremediably "lost face" over its claims concerning Jiddu Krishnamurti, a young Hindu whom Mrs. Besant adopted, asserting him to be the incarnation of the expected World Teacher, and widely announcing him as their Messiah. His teachings, purporting to have been received from the Great Teacher are recorded in his book, *At the Feet of the Master*. Vast gatherings were held in Ommen, Holland, which he made his headquarters. In 1928 he was still convinced of his divine mission, and as reported in *The New York Sun*, April 9, said, "I am the voice of the Great Teacher. I have the Spirit. You may not believe it. I don't care; it makes no difference to me." In 1931, however, much to the dismay of his devotees, he publicly renounced his Messianic pretensions. "I am not an actor," he said, "I refuse to wear the robes of a Messiah." The Order of the Star of the East which sponsored him has been disbanded.

With the above documented statements before him, the Christian is in a position to form an estimate of this cult. Its heathen and Spiritistic origin, the character of its founders, the antichristian nature of its doctrines, and the abdication of its heralded Messiah, combine to convince that the whole movement is not of God, and should be both shunned and exposed.

IX

CHRISTADELPHIANISM

THE author has good reason to regard this heresy as a dangerous counterfeit. In the days when the "Keswick" Movement had its beginnings—about 1875—his grandparents were keen and zealous Christians, rejoicing in full salvation. Each morning the grandfather could be heard walking up and down the drawing-room singing F. R. Havergal's consecration hymn ere the work of the day began. In their thirst for Bible knowledge they were somehow brought into touch with some Christadelphians who were very diligent Bible students. Bibles were brought out in the evenings, and studied until the early hours of the morning. Soon they became zealous propagators of the "new light" which had come to them. Some time later, the grandmother perceived where she had been led astray and utterly renounced Christadelphianism and all its works, but not until her excursion into this false faith had exerted a tragic effect on some members of her family. The grandfather never withdrew from their communion, but lost all the glow and promise of his earlier years, although he was never a thoroughly "orthodox" Christadelphian.

That the following is a substantially correct setting forth of the Christadelphian beliefs is borne out by a letter received when this study first appeared in a magazine. The writer of the letter, a Christadelphian of forty years' standing, said, "In the main, and as far as it goes, you have fairly stated our beliefs, with two exceptions." The present article has been amended to correct the two points to which exception was taken.

CHARACTERISTICS

Two of their outstanding characteristics are:

Zeal

The zeal with which they pursue their study is worthy of a
better cause, and might well be emulated by those of us who,
while perceiving their errors, give so little time to searching
of the Scriptures. And their zeal is no less evident in their
"compassing land and sea to make one proselyte." A pros-
pective convert is most assiduously cultivated, and does not
easily escape their clutches. It is noticeable, however, that
they are not outstanding in their zeal in endeavouring to
reach the outcasts and sinful of our cities.

Intolerance

In common with other cults, the adherents of this one un-
church all others. In *Who are Christadelphians?* pp. 3, 6, 8,
the following passages occur: "Convinced that this is the
only Scriptural constitution of the 'one body,' of which Jesus
Christ is alone the head, and Who has no personal representative
on earth, we repudiate the popular churches, and all their
adjuncts, as no part thereof, and affirm that *there is no salvation within the pale of any of them.* For we hold that the
religious opinions and sacramentalism of all orders and classes
of men in 'Christendom' so-called are nothing more than that
'strong delusion' sent of God upon all mankind that they should
believe a lie, that they might all be condemned. *We object to
the fundamental doctrines of Christendom;* the religion of the
churches and chapels is a negation of Bible teaching on almost
all points. We hold it to be 'the abominations of the earth'
with all dissenting names and denominations, aggregately
styled 'names of blasphemy,' of which the European body
politic, symbolised by the eight-headed, scarlet-coloured beast
is said to be 'full' (Rev. 17: 3)."

Let us now consider their

CREED

From the above quotation it is seen that Christadelphianism
denies all the doctrines which the Church holds as essential
to the Christian faith. While posing as its champions, they
are in reality among the greatest enemies of the truth, a
statement which we shall proceed to prove.

The Trinity

Christadelphianism denies the Scriptural doctrine of the Trinity. "There were not two or three eternal persons before 'the man Christ Jesus,' but ONE—God the Father, whose relation to the Son was afterwards exemplified in the event related by Luke (1: 35), by which was established what Paul styles 'the mystery of godliness' (1 Tim. 3: 16)." "Jesus Christ, the Son of God, is not the 'second person' of an eternal Trinity of Gods, but the manifestation of the ONE ETERNAL CREATOR."

In this way the teaching of the Church on the Trinity is travestied. What intelligent believer has ever thought of "an eternal Trinity of Gods," which would be but a form of polytheism?

For answer, see Isa. 63: 8–10; Matt. 28: 19.

Jesus Christ

Christadelphianism denies that Christ is the eternal, incarnate Son of God.

"Jesus had no existence prior to His birth by Mary."

"Jesus is the name of the virgin's Son, and not that of an eternally pre-existent God Who came down from heaven, and in some mysterious way became incarnate in the Flesh."[1]

"The Father was manifest in the flesh, not a pre-existent co-eternal Son, which is impossible."[2]

"The Son is a manifestation of the Father in a man begotten by the Spirit."[3]

"That Christ's nature was immaculate" is among the doctrines to be rejected.[4]

Quoting Rom. 8: 3, R. Roberts says,[5] "It was the same flesh, full of the same propensities, and the same desires, in Christ as in us; for sinful flesh and the likeness of sinful flesh mean the same thing."

"Deriving from His mother both the propensities that lead to sin and the sentence of death that was passed because of sin, He was absolutely sinless as to disobedience, whilst subject to the impulses and consequences of sin. For it was

[1] *Is It Blasphemy?*, p. 19.
[2] Walker, *Truth about the Trinity*, p. 13.
[3] R. Roberts, *Christendom Astray*, p. 108.
[4] *Constitution of the Christadelphian Ecclesia*, p. 13.
[5] *The Slain Lamb*, p. 21.

necessary that He should appear in the nature of Abraham and David, which was sinful nature."[1]

"Christadelphians do not worship the Lord Jesus Christ in the same way that they worship the Father."[2]

Further quotations from their literature are unnecessary to establish that they deny His eternal Sonship and deity, leaving us with a sinful Christ, who came "under the beneficial operation of His own death."

In this connection, D. M. Panton wrote, "The Jews stumbled nineteen hundred years ago exactly where the Christadelphians stumble today. 'And they said, Is not this Jesus, the son of Joseph, whose father and mother we know? How doth He now say, I am come out of heaven' (John 6: 42). Awful and eternal is the answer of the Lord. 'Except ye believe that I am He'—the pre-existent One—'ye shall die in your sins' (John 8: 24). The pre-existence of the Eternal Son of God is a matter of life and death. No one who denies our Lord's deity can be forgiven (John 5: 23)."

For answer, see John 1: 1–3, 14; 8: 58; 17: 5; 20: 28; Rom. 9: 5; Heb. 1: 3, 6, 8.

The Holy Spirit

Christadelphianism denies the personality of the Spirit.

"The Spirit is not a personal God distinct from the Father, but the radiant invisible power or energy from the Father, filling universal space and forming the medium of His omniscient perceptions, and the instrument of His omnipotent behests, whether in creation or inspiration."

For answer, see Matt. 28: 19; John 7: 39; 14: 16, 17, 26; 15: 26; 16: 7, 13; 1 Cor. 12: 11.

The Devil

Christadelphianism denies the existence of a personal devil.

"The Devil is not (as is commonly supposed) a personal supernatural agent of evil, and in fact there is no such being in existence. The devil is a scriptural manifestation of sin in the flesh in its several phases of manifestation . . . after the style of metaphor which speaks of wisdom as a woman, riches as mammon and Satan as God of this world, sin as a master, etc."

---

[1] *Blood of Christ*, p. 26.
[2] *Is It Blasphemy?*, p. 19.

For answer, see Job 1: 6–12; Zech. 3: 1–2; Matt. 4: 1–11; Acts 5: 3; Rev. 20: 1–3.

The Atonement

Christadelphianism emasculates the doctrine of the sub-stitutionary atonement of Christ.

"The idea that Christ has borne our punishment and paid our debts, and that His righteousness is placed to our credit, and that all we have to do is to believe it, is demoralising. Blighting results are to be witnessed in all communities where the doctrine of a substitutionary sacrifice and an imputed righteousness holds sway."[1]

"Christ has given no satisfaction, paid no debt."[2]

"If the blood of Christ could be found, it would not be of any spiritual value."[3]

"The death of Christ was not to appease the wrath of an offended Deity, but to express the love of the Father in a necessary sacrifice for sin, that the law of sin and death . . . might be nullified."

For answer, see Isa. 53: 5; Matt. 20: 28; Rom. 5: 9; 1 Cor. 15: 3; 2 Cor. 5: 21; 1 Pet. 2: 24; 3: 18; 1 John 1: 7.

Heaven

"Earth, and not 'heaven above the skies,' is the inheritance of the saints."

"The belief in question is not only erroneous in supposing that the dead go to such places as the popular heaven or hell *immediately after death, but in thinking that they ever go there at any time.*"

"This going to heaven is a purely gratuitous speculation."[4]

For answer, see Luke 23: 43; John 14: 1–3; 2 Cor. 5: 8; Phil. 2: 23; 1 Thess. 4: 17.

Hell

Christadelphianism denies the doctrine of the eternal future punishment of the wicked, and for it they substitute a system of conditional immortality.

[1] R. Roberts, *The Blood of Christ*, p. 29.
[2] R. Roberts, *The Slain Lamb*, p. 21.
[3] *The Blood of Christ*, p. 7.
[4] Roberts, *Christendom Astray*, pp. 44, 45.

"It also follows of necessity that the popular theory of hell and 'eternal torments' is a fiction."

"Death, the extinction of being, is the predetermined issue of a sinful course."

"We are explicitly informed by other testimonies, that while *aionian* punishment ends in death, the life to be conferred in that same *aion* is extinguishable."[1]

Mr. A. J. Pollock makes the following cryptic comment on this statement: "That is to say that *aionian*, the Greek adjective for eternal, means eternal in one part of the verse, and not in the other part of the verse. What confidence can the reader have in any reasoning of Mr. Roberts, or indeed in his honesty, when he can make words suit his fancy, and call white black and black white."

For answer, see Matt. 10: 28; 25: 46; Luke 12: 4, 5; 16: 19–31; Rev. 20: 10–15.

Baptism

Christadelphianism denies the validity of any baptism other than their own.

"We recognise as brethren and welcome to our fellowship, all who have been immersed *after their acceptance of our doctrines and precepts*."

Among doctrines to be rejected is, "That a knowledge of the (Christadelphian) truth is not necessary to make baptism valid."[2]

"Baptism by water is the ceremony by which believing men and women are united to Christ, and constituted heirs of the life everlasting."

To them, baptism is essential to salvation. "To such (believers) it (baptism) is the means of that present union with Christ, which is preparatory to perfect assimilation at the resurrection. It is, therefore, necessary to salvation."

"A man may believe in all the glorious promises of God, and yet not be a participator in them. *He must be baptized*."[3]

For answer, see John 3: 36; 1 Pet. 3: 20, 21; 1 John 5: 13.

Salvation

Christadelphians promulgate a doctrine of autosoterism.

"The belief of the Gospel described by the Spirit of God as

[1] Roberts, *Christendom Astray*, pp. 49, 68.
[2] *Constitution of the Christadelphian Ecclesia*, pp. 1–13.
[3] Roberts, *Christendom Astray*, pp. 119, 302.

'the things concerning the kingdom of God and the name of Jesus Christ,' together with baptism, and the obedience to the commandments of Christ, are indispensable to eternal life."[1]

"To sum up the whole matter, a person instructed in 'the word of the kingdom,' enquiring what must he do to be saved, has only one Scriptural answer to receive: 'Repent and be baptised into the name of Jesus Christ for the remission of sins' (Acts 2: 38). When he has yielded this 'obedience of faith,' he is 'born of water' through the inceptive influence of the truth; and having entered 'The Name,' his sins are 'covered'; his transgression 'hid'; his whole past life is cancelled, and he has commenced a life of probation in which he is a lawful candidate for that 'birth of the Spirit' from the grave which will finally constitute him a 'son of God, being the children of the resurrection' (Luke 20: 36). . . . *But his ultimate acceptance will depend upon the character he develops in this new relation.*"[2] (Italics ours).

The best Christadelphianism can offer a sinner bowed beneath a burden of sin, is yet another period of probation. No assurance of salvation is theirs.

For answer, see Rom. 3: 24, 28; 4: 4, 5; Eph. 2: 8, 9.

Thus Christadelphianism, on its own statements, is proved to be a counterfeit of true Christianity. It substitutes a modified Unitarianism for Trinitarianism; it robs Christ of His pre-existence and deity and sinlessness; degrades the Holy Spirit to the level of an impersonal power; denies personality to the Devil; caricatures the atonement, denies eternal punishment, and leaves us to take care of our own salvation.

Who that knows "the truth as it is in Jesus" would be prepared to barter it for such an empty and heartless tissue of negations?

[1] *Bible Fingerposts*, p. 243.
[2] Roberts, *Christendom Astray*, p. 306.

X

MORMONISM OR THE CHURCH OF JESUS CHRIST OF LATTER-DAY SAINTS

NUMERICALLY, Mormonism is the largest of the cults, with a membership in 1960 of 1,650,000 in all its branches. This shows an increase of no less than 30 per cent during the previous decade. Magnificent and costly temples have been erected in places as widely separated as Los Angeles and New Zealand. Their missionary activities are prodigious, more than 7,500 younger men actively propagating their religion throughout the world—and doing it in the main at their own expense. We have no quarrel with Mormons as individuals, for many of them live exemplary lives, but this must not blind us to the error and even the blasphemy of their doctrine.

ORIGIN OF MORMONISM

The story of the rise and history of this cult makes tremendous demands on the credulity of the normal man. The name most prominently associated with the movement is that of *Joseph Smith*, an illiterate young man who, according to his own mother, was hardly able to read until manhood, and knew practically nothing of the Bible. He was unfortunate in his parentage, for his father and mother, both of them ignorant and fanatical, laid great emphasis on the relevance of dreams and visions. And who knows but that his subsequent career was not the self-fulfilment of their prophecy that their son Joseph would found a new religion?

Concerning Joseph Smith, Dr. Edmund Fairfield, President of Michigan College, wrote when in Palmyra, N.Y.: "Three were mentioned to me who had been intimately acquainted with Joseph Smith from the age of ten years to twenty-five and upwards. The testimony of these men was given under no stress of any kind. It was clear, decided, unequivocal testimony in which they all agreed. 'Joseph Smith is simply a notorious liar.' 'The things for which Joseph was most notorious were his vulgar speech and his life of unspeakable lewdness.' "

Through some fortuitous circumstance he was thrown into contact with an unfrocked Baptist minister, Sidney Rigdon, who had subsequently thrown in his lot with the Campbellites until he fell foul of Campbell. Rigdon conceived the idea that if Campbell could secure such a following he could become still more famous by going beyond the Bible and giving the world a totally new revelation. In Joseph Smith he found a ready instrument and willing collaborator. The fruit of this unholy union was *The Book of Mormon.*

Their story was that on September 21, 1823, Smith had an angel visitant, Moroni by name, who revealed to him that in A.D. 420 there had been secreted in the hill Cumorah, near Palmyra, N.Y., several golden plates on which was inscribed the history of the Nephites who came to America from Jerusalem in 600 B.C. Joseph, who had early evinced a penchant for occultism, went to the spot, and there were the golden plates and a large pair of spectacles—Urim and Thummin he called them—by the aid of which he was enabled to decipher and translate into English the mystic hieroglyphics, which he claimed were "Reformed Egyptian."

Concerning this claim Professor Charles Anthon, a noted linguist, made the following comment: "A very brief investigation convinced me that it was a mere hoax, and a very clumsy one too. The characters were arranged in columns like the Chinese mode of writing, and presented the most singular medley I have ever beheld. Greek, Hebrew, and all sorts of letters more or less distorted, either through unskilfulness or from actual design, were intermingled with sundry delineations of half-moons, stars and other natural objects, and the whole ended in a rude representation of the Mexican zodiac."

In this connection, Horton Davies writes: "Our mystification at the linguistic expertness of this illiterate man is increased by the assurance of egyptlogists that Egyptian hieroglyphics remained unchanged from the fifth century B.C. until the fourth century A.D. Furthermore, not only is 'Reformed Egyptian' unknown to the egyptologists, but these experts themselves were unable to decipher Egyptian inscriptions until the discovery of the Rosetta stone. We are left to judge between a gigantic fraud and a great miracle, as the explanation of these events."[1]

The true story is as follows: A Presbyterian preacher, Solomon Spaulding by name, wrote an imaginary history of the people who inhabited America in the early days, entitled *The Manuscript Found*. His effort not being accepted for publication, he left it with a printer at Pittsburgh, Patterson by name, and died two years later. The aforementioned Rigdon, who frequented Patterson's shop, came on the old manuscript, in which he saw a short-cut to fame. With this as a basis, he compiled *The Book of Mormon*, and with the help of Parley P. Pratt and Joseph Smith, perpetrated one of the greatest religious hoaxes of the century. Pratt was a worthy companion for Smith, coming to an untimely end when he was shot by an enraged husband whose wife Pratt had seduced and taken to Utah as one of his wives.

The degree of credulity required to accept the Mormon version of the origin of their holy book seems inexplicable unless it be that, "because they received not the love of the truth . . . God sent them strong delusion, that they should believe a lie" (2 Thess. 2: 10, 11).

After Joseph Smith's death at the hand of an infuriated armed mob at Carthage in 1844, his place of leadership was assumed by *Brigham Young*, who led the immigration of the Mormons to Utah, in order to escape the arm of the law. He died thirty years later, leaving a fortune of £400,000, seventeen wives (eight had preceded him in death), and fifty-six children.

Mention must here be made of "The Reorganized Church of Jesus Christ of Latter-Day Saints," or "Josephites," one of the offshoots of the Mother Church. When Brigham Young was elected to the leadership, a minority, loyal to the Smith family, maintained that Joseph's son was the rightful successor. They accordingly broke away, setting up rival headquarters at Wisconsin in 1853. To their credit be it said that they denounced polygamy, which doctrine they attributed to Young, and renounced the orthodox "Adam-God" teaching. The reorganized church, however, has not made great headway.

Such in brief is the origin of the movement and the history of some of its leaders.

[1] *Christian Deviations*, p. 74.

If it be asked why Mormonism should be classed as a heresy, the answer is threefold:

It is Antichristian. While concealing its errors under the terminology of Christianity, it either perverts or denies all the fundamental truths of Christianity. God is a man of flesh— Adam. Christ's atonement has to do only with the sins of Adam. Salvation is by works, and through baptism. Christ is the Son of the Adam-God and Mary, not born of the Virgin. The Holy Spirit is a divine fluid. Sin was necessary. All these points are substantiated later from their own writings.

It is Anti-moral. Polygamy was practised among Mormons at least from the time of the first public announcement of the "doctrine" in Utah in 1852.[1] It is true that after a protracted legal battle the practice was officially abandoned in 1889, but it has been surreptitiously and sporadically indulged until even so recent a date as 1944, when American law enforcement officers simultaneously arrested forty-six members of the Fundamentalist sect of the Mormons in Utah, Idaho and Arizona.[2] In an interview with the Salt Lake *Telegram* on this subject, Mrs. Rhea A. Kunz said, "Of course we believe in what we are doing. This thing is far bigger than the individual, for it inevitably will encompass much more than the man-made laws by which the world lives and will become a fundamental component in the lives of all right-living people."[3] The writer has personally asked senior Mormon missionaries concerning the teaching of their church on polygamy and has received the reply that while they still believe in it, because it is contrary to State laws, they do not practise it.

Whatever the practice of the various sects of present-day Mormons, it cannot be gainsaid that the advocacy of polygamy has not been expunged from the official and sacred books of the cult. Here are Joseph Smith's words appearing in the 1944 edition of *Doctrine and Covenants*: "If any man espouse a virgin, and desire to espouse another, and the first give her consent, and if he espouse the second, and they are virgins, and have bowed to no other man, then he is justified; he

---

[1] *Wife*, No. 19, p. 65.
[2] *Newsweek.*
[3] Van Baalen, *Chaos of Cults*, p. 162.

cannot commit adultery for they are given to him; for he cannot commit adultery with that that belongeth unto him and unto no one else. And if he have ten virgins given unto him by this law, he cannot commit adultery, for they belong to him, and they are given unto him; therefore he is justified."[1]

Joseph Smith's successor was no less explicit in his advocacy of plurality of wives: "Now if any of you deny the plurality of wives and continue to do so, I promise that you will be damned; and I will go still further and say, take this revelation, or any other revelation that the Lord has given, and deny it in your feelings, and I promise that you will be damned. But the saints who live their religion will be exalted."[2]

And all this in spite of such Scriptures as "Neither shall he multiply wives unto himself" (Deut. 17 : 17). "A bishop must be blameless, the husband of one wife" (1 Tim. 3 : 2). "Let the deacons be the husbands of one wife" (1 Tim. 3 : 12). "Ordain elders . . . the husband of one wife" (Tit. 1 : 5, 6).

In addition to the ordinary marriage vows which are binding only until death, Mormonism superadds celestial marriage or spiritual wifery. It is taught that sex relationship continues in the eternal state. "The eternal union of the sexes," said Parley P. Pratt, one of the early elders, "in and after the resurrection, is mainly for the purpose of renewing and continuing the work of procreation."[3]

"Except a man and his wife enter into an everlasting covenant and be married for eternity, while in this probation, by the power and authority of the Holy Priesthood, they will cease to increase when they die, that is, they will not have any children after the resurrection. But those who are married by the power and authority of the Priesthood in this life, and continue without committing the sin against the Holy Ghost, will continue to increase and have children in the celestial glory."[4] Thus the word of man is elevated above the word of Christ who said, "But they which shall be accounted worthy to obtain that world and the resurrection from the dead, neither marry nor are given in marriage" (Luke 20 : 34, 35). "In the resurrection they neither marry nor are

[1] Doctrine and Covenants, Sec. 132, pp. 4, 61, 62.
[2] Brigham Young at the Bowery, Provo, Utah, July 14, 1855.
[3] Key to Theology (1943), p. 167.
[4] Priesthood and Covenant (1939), p. 43.

given in marriage, but are as the angels of God in heaven"
(Matt. 22: 30). The Mormon misinterpretation of these verses
is that they refer to those who have not gone through the
special form of celestial marriage.[1]

Much could be said under this heading. While the reorganized
church repudiates polygamy, even they cannot deny that it
was practised by all their original twelve apostles. The fact
that polygamy was tolerated at all is sufficient to condemn
the whole system.

It is anti-democratic. "The Kingdom of God (or Mormon
priesthood) is an order of government established by Divine
authority. . . . All other governments are illegal and unauthorised. All people attempting to govern themselves by
laws of their own making and by officers of their own
appointment, are in direct rebellion against the Kingdom of
God."[2]

They make the bold claim that the priesthood (Mormon)
holds the power and right to give laws and commandments to
individuals, churches, rulers, nations and the world, to appoint
kings, presidents, governors or judges, a claim certainly not
lacking in modesty.

The spectacular growth of the movement finds its cause, in
part, in the virile and vigorous leadership it has enjoyed since
its earliest days. Its leaders have ever been dynamic men of
foresight and no mean executive ability. Its autocratic
organization has been superb. The very persecutions they have
endured have gained for their doctrines a sympathetic ear,
while their "miracles of healing" drew many adherents from
the ranks of suffering humanity. Today, radio audiences the
world over are accustomed to hear Alexander Shriner at the
organ, J. Spencer Cornwall leading the beautiful choir, and
Richard Evans giving the spoken word. This popular broadcast has gained them a great deal of goodwill from a public
which is ignorant of the deadly poison which lies behind the
honeyed words.

COUNTERFEITS OF MORMONISM

Among the counterfeits of this cult we may enumerate
three:

[1] Richards, *A Marvellous Work*, pp. 205, 206.
[2] *Orson Pratt's Works*, p. 41.

A Counterfeit Bible. The Book of Mormon, the origin of which has been already indicated. Among many proofs of its spurious nature, we may point out these convincing facts. Of those who witnessed to the authenticity of the book, the first three, Cowdry, Whitmer and Harris were given three days to clear out of the church, and were denounced by Mormons as thieves, liars and blacklegs, conspiring to deceive and cheat the saints of their property. Three of the second group of witnesses later repudiated Mormonism. Again, to anyone familiar with the Campbellite doctrines and phraseology, the presence of their peculiar tenets and expressions in the book is to say the least suspicious.

Another interesting though condemning fact is that the hundreds of direct quotations from Old and New Testaments are all from the Authorised Version, although the golden plates were written twelve hundred years before King James authorised that version! It abounds in modern words, expressions and discoveries. Words very akin to Shakespeare's well-known phrase, "the undiscovered country from whose bourne no traveller returns," were used in 2 Nephi 1 : 28, two thousand years before Shakespeare's birth!

There are also verbatim quotations from the seventeenth-century Westminster *Confession of Faith* and an excerpt from a Methodist book of discipline. Numerous anachronisms are also embodied. A year after the publication of *The Book of Mormon,* Alexander Campbell observed that in the book supposedly completed in A.D. 421, Smith had written "every error and almost every truth discussed in New York for the last ten years. He decides all the great controversies—infant baptism, ordination, the Trinity . . . and even the question of freemasonry, republican government and the rights of man."[1]

It remains to be said that the purported history of *The Book of Mormon* finds not one scintilla of support from the investigations of disinterested anthropologists. Such is the Mormon Bible which is given equal if not superior authority to the Bible as we have it.

A Counterfeit Apostolate. The Mormons do not claim apostolic succession, but apostolic restoration, since all other priesthoods save their own have failed. They have their twelve apostles. If as exhorted in Rev. 2 : 2 we "try them that call themselves apostles, and are not," we find them wanting, for the Scriptural requirements for apostleship are: acquaintance with Christ before crucifixion; seeing Christ after His resurrection; reception of commission direct from Him, the Head of the Church; ability to work miracles.

Judged by these standards, "such men are false prophets, deceitful workers, fashioning themselves into the apostles of Christ" (2 Cor. 11: 13).

A Counterfeit Priesthood. Their priesthood alone has divine authority to act for God and is answerable only to God, and their followers implicitly bow to their dictates. And yet there is no recognition among them that in Christ our High Priest all priesthood was fully and for ever fulfilled, and that every believer now forms part of a Kingdom of priests.

CREED OF MORMONISM

But whatever the character of its founders, it is the nature of its doctrines which is of supreme importance. How do they square with those of the evangelical Church?

The Trinity

"We believe in God the Eternal Father, and His Son Jesus Christ, and in the Holy Ghost."[1]

There is surely nothing exceptionable in this statement if the words mean what they appear to mean. But do they? Who is the God of Mormonism? Who is His Son? Who is the Holy Ghost?

God

Unlike Christian Science, which gives us an impersonal God, Mormonism degrades Him to the level of a magnified man. "God himself was once as we are now, and is an exalted man, and sits enthroned in yonder heavens; it is the first principle of the Gospel to know that He was once a man like us" (Joseph Smith).

To a Mormon, God is Adam. "When our Father Adam came into the Garden of Eden, he came into it with a celestial body, and brought Eve, one of his wives with him. . . . He is our Father and our God, and the only God with whom we

[1] *Articles of Faith.*

have to do."[1] It is only fair to say in the words of W. P. Walters that, "These one-time gems of heavenly light are looked upon by many modern Mormons as the unwise 'speculations' of the early leaders." But this is still generally taught today.

"We believe in the plurality of Gods."[2]

"God created man as we create our children: for there is no other process of creation."[3]

"The Father has a body of flesh and bones . . . and the Son also; but the Holy Ghost has not a body of flesh and bones but is a personage of spirit."[4]

"In heaven where our spirits were born there are many Gods, each of whom has his own wife or wives, which were given to him previous to his redemption, while yet in his mortal state."[5]

That these teachings are still those of Mormonism will be clear from a perusal of *A Marvellous Work and a Wonder* by Le Grand Richards (1950).

For answer, see Deut. 6: 4; Hos. 11: 9; Matt. 22: 24–30; Mark 12: 24, 32; John 4: 24.

Christ

"When the Virgin Mary conceived the child Jesus, the Father had begotten him in his own likeness. He was not begotten of the Holy Ghost. And who is the Father? He is the first of the human family. . . ."[6]

"His unique status in the flesh as the offspring of a mortal mother and of an immortal, or resurrected and glorified Father."[7]

"The fleshly body of Jesus required a mother as well as a father. Therefore, the father and mother of Jesus according to the flesh must have been associated together in the capacity of husband and wife; hence the Virgin Mary must have been for the time being the lawful wife of God the Father."[8]

[1] Brigham Young, *Journal of Discourses*, Vol. I, p. 50.
[2] *Mormon Doctrine of Deity*, p. 11.
[3] *Journal of Discourses*, Vol. II, p. 122.
[4] *Doctrines and Covenants*, p. 462.
[5] Orson Pratt, *The Seer*, Vol. I, p. 37.
[6] *Journal of Discourses*, Vol. I, p. 50.
[7] *Articles of Faith* (1925 edition), pp. 472–3.
[8] *The Seer*, p. 159.

"Now remember from this time forth, and for ever, that Jesus Christ was not begotten by the Holy Ghost. . . . I was in conversation with a certain learned professor on this subject, when I replied to this idea— 'If the Son was begotten by the Holy Ghost, it would be very dangerous to baptize and confirm females and give the Holy Ghost to them, lest he should beget children to be palmed upon the Elders of the people, bringing the Elders into great difficulties.' "[1]

"We say it was Jesus Christ who was married (at Cana) to the Marys and Martha, whereby He could see His seed before He was crucified."[2]

"If He was never married, His intimacy with Mary and Martha, and the other Mary also, must have been highly unbecoming and improper, to say the best of it."[3]

For answer, see Matt. 1: 18; Luke 1: 35.

The Holy Ghost

"The Holy Ghost is a personage of spirit in the form of man . . . and hence confined in his personage to a definite space."[4]

"Jesus Christ . . . was filled with a divine substance or fluid, called the Holy Spirit."[5]

Joseph Smith differentiated between the identity and functions of the Holy Ghost and the Holy Spirit."[6]

"The purest, most refined and subtle of all these substances (such as electricity, galvanism, magnetism) . . . is that substance called the Holy Spirit."[7] "Divine fluid."

For answer, see John 4: 24; 14: 17; 16: 13, 14, 15; Acts 13: 2; 16: 6; 1 John 5: 7.

From the above quotations it is abundantly clear that though Mormons use much the same terminology as evangelicals concerning the Trinity, the words used have an exactly antithetical content. "Mormonism seeks to reduce God to a carnal plane and even ascribes to Him human methods of reproduction fully in keeping with the immoral and polygamous characters of Smith and Young who had forty-eight and

---

[1] *Journal of Discourses*, Vol. I, p. 51.
[2] Orson Hyde, *Journal*, Vol. II, p. 80.
[3] Ibid., Vol. IV, p. 259.
[4] *A Marvellous Work and Wonder*, p. 120.
[5] *Key to Theology* (5th edition), p. 38.
[6] S. L. Richards, *Contributions of Joseph Smith*.
[7] *Key to Science of Theology*, p. 39.

twenty-five wives respectively, and the latter, fifty-six children."[1]

Man

"We believe that men will be punished for their own sins and not for Adam's transgression."[2]

The pre-existence of man is taught. "Life's meaning can best be unravelled by searching man's inmost nature. In that pursuit the most fundamental discovery is the eternal existence of man—that man lived before he came upon earth. In that pre-existent life he thought, acted and progressed, even as, in a different degree, and under a different environment, he does upon earth."[3]

"The spirits of all men were in the beginning with God."[4]

"What God was once, we are now; what God is now, we shall be" (Brigham Young). "They who have obeyed the laws of the Gospel . . . shall have thrones, dominion and endless increase; they shall be Gods creating and governing worlds and peopling them with their own offspring."[5]

For answer, see Gen. 1: 27; John 1: 18.

Sin

"Tied inseparably to the Mormon concept of deity is the Mormon idea of salvation. For the most part the Biblical doctrine of sin is replaced with the idea of sins (for example, smoking, drinking alcohol, coffee, tea) none of which merit everlasting punishment."[6]

"Was it necessary that Adam should partake of the forbidden fruit? Yes, unless he had done so, he would not have known good and evil here, neither could he have mortal posterity."[7] "We ought to consider the fall of our first parents as one of the great steps to eternal exaltation and happiness."[8] "Adam and Eve rejoiced and praised God, when they sinned."

---

[1] Martin, *Rise of the Cults*, p. 52.
[2] *Articles of Faith*.
[3] Widtsoe, *Life's Meaning*, p. 1.
[4] *A Marvellous Work*, p. 287.
[5] *Manual*, 1901–1902, Part I, p. 52.
[6] W. P. Walters in *Christianity Today*, Vol. V, No. 6, p. 229.
[7] *Mormon Catechism*.
[8] Ibid.

For answer, see Gen. 2: 7; Rom. 5: 12; 6: 23; 8: 7; 1 Jas. 1: 8.

Atonement

"We believe that through the atonement of Jesus Christ all mankind may be saved, by obedience to the laws and ordinances of the Gospel."[1]

They first rob Christ of His power to offer atonement by classing Him as a polygamist, son of the Adam-God and Mary, and then claim to believe that through His atonement mankind may be saved. What atonement could such a being make? In any case, say they, the atonement of Christ does not save souls, but only delivers the earth from the power of death.

"What was lost in Adam was restored in Christ. . . . Transgressions of the law brought death upon all the posterity of Adam, the restoration through the atonement restored all the human family to life. . . . The atonement made by Jesus Christ resulted in the resurrection of the human body."[2]

"The special or individual effect of the atonement makes it possible for any and every soul to obtain absolution from the dread effect of personal sins, through the mediation of Christ; but such saving intercession is to be invoked by individual effort as manifested through faith, repentance and continued works of righteousness. . . . Now, that the blessing of redemption from individual sins, while free for all to attain, is nevertheless conditioned on individual effort, is as plainly declared as is the truth of unconditional redemption from the effects of the Fall."[3]

For answer, see Acts 13: 39; Rom. 4: 25; Gal. 1: 4.

Salvation

"Redemption from personal sins can only be obtained through obedience to the requirements of the Gospel (Mormon ceremonies) and a life of good works." "He that receives the message (of *The Book of Mormon*) and endures to the end shall be saved; he that rejects it shall be damned."[4] Thus, the atonement of Christ is nullified, and salvation reduced to a

[1] *Articles of Faith.*
[2] Taylor, *The Mediation and The Atonement,* pp. 170, 177, 178.
[3] Talmadge, *Articles of Faith,* pp. 90, 92.
[4] *Pratt's Works,* Paper I.

system of good works plus a belief in the fraud of Joseph Smith.

"The gospel of Jesus Christ is called the plan of salvation. It is a system of rules by complying with which salvation may be obtained."[1]

"The sectarian dogma of justification by faith alone, has exercised an influence for evil since the early days of Christianity."[2]

For answer, see Rom. 5: 1; Eph. 2: 8, 9; Tit. 3: 5, 6.

Ordinances

"We believe that the first principles and ordinances of the Bible are: First, Faith in our Lord Jesus Christ; second, Repentance; third, Baptism by immersion for the remission of sins; fourth, Laying on of hands for the Gift of the Holy Ghost."[3]

Baptism

The Cerinthian heresy of baptism for the dead is perpetuated. "A man may be baptised as proxy for and in behalf of the dead."[4] "Baptism is necessary to salvation."[5]

For answer, see 1 Cor. 1: 14 with 1 Cor. 4: 15. Note the careful wording of Mark 16: 16.

The Church

The Mormon church claims to be the only authentic church of God, restored by God and Christ in person, by angels, and by Peter, James and John.

"The Lord provided that salvation should come through His gospel functioning through his Church wherein are prophets and apostles. . . .

"Is there such a Church upon the earth? Until a little more than a hundred years ago, there was not. . . . But a hundred years ago the Almighty restored his true Church to the earth again. He has raised up modern prophets and apostles to direct the work."[6]

[1] Elder E. F. Parry, *The Scrap Book*.
[2] *Articles of Faith*.
[3] *Articles of Faith*.
[4] *House of the Lord*, p. 77.
[5] Talmadge, *Articles of Faith*, p. 130.
[6] M. E. Petersen, *Which Is Right ?*, p. 16.

"We believe in the same organisation that existed in the primitive church, namely apostles, prophets, pastors, teachers, evangelists, etc."[1]

"All the churches preach false doctrine and are under the curse of God" (Orson Pratt). "All the creeds were an abomination in my sight, corrupt professors. . . ."[2]

The Devil

"Thus we see that Lucifer, the son of the morning, is our elder brother and the brother of Jesus Christ, but he rebelled against God and was cast down from heaven with his angels."[3]

Miracles

"We believe in the gift of tongues, prophecy, revelation, visions, healing, etc."[4]

"Contemporary evidence proves that the supernatural was really present among the early Mormons," says D. M. Panton. "In the first two years of the sect, citizens of Jackson County issued a statement in which they refer to the 'contemptible gibberish with which they habitually profane the sabbath and which they dignify with the appellation of unknown tongues'."[5] They regard miracles as the credentials of the Christian, and the fact (?) that they are possessed by every Mormon and not by others proves Mormonism the only true religion.

For answer, see 2 Thess. 2: 9–11; Rev. 16: 14.

The Scriptures

"We believe the Bible to be the Word of God, so far as it is correctly translated; we also believe the *Book of Mormon* to be the Word of God."[6] In practice, the *Book of Mormon* receives higher honour than the Bible.

To the Mormons the Bible is not the sole and infallible Word of God but only a convenient tool to forward their subtle and misleading teaching. Their recourse to the Bible

---

[1] *Articles of Faith.*
[2] *The Mormons*, p. 24.
[3] Address in Utah, by Elder Andrew Jensen, *Desert News*, January 26, 1928.
[4] *Articles of Faith.*
[5] *The Mormons*, p. 69.
[6] *Articles of Faith.*

serves to give an aura of orthodoxy to teachings which are absolutely heterodox.

"If it be admitted that the apostles and evangelists did write the books of the New Testament, that does not prove of itself that they were divinely inspired at the time they wrote."[1]

"Thou fool that shall say, A Bible, A Bible, we have got a Bible, and we need no more Bible. . . . Wherefore murmur ye, because ye shall receive more of my word."[2]

"And whatsoever they ('those ordained unto the priesthood') shall speak when moved upon by the Holy Ghost, shall be scripture, shall be the will of the Lord, shall be the mind of the Lord, shall be the Word of the Lord . . . and the power of God unto salvation."[3]

"Wilford Woodruff is a prophet . . . and he can make Scriptures as good as those in the Bible" (Apostle J. W. Taylor, Conference, Salt Lake, April 5, 1897). "The living oracles (modern priestly revelations), are worth more to the Latter-Day Saints than all the Bibles."

Concerning the writings of Joseph Smith, Stephen L. Richards writes, "His literary labours must not be forgotten. He produced more Scripture, that is the revealed word of God, than any other man of whom we have record. Indeed his total scriptural production would almost equal those of all others put together."[4]

Hell

"The false doctrine that the punishment to be visited upon erring souls is endless . . . must be regarded as one of the most pernicious results of misapprehension of Scripture. It is a dogma of unauthorised and erring sectaries. . . ."[5]

If ever St. Paul's pronouncement concerning the Judaizing heresy (Gal. 1 : 9) was applicable to any group, it is appropriate to Mormonism, for there is no identity whatever between Paul's Gospel and that of the Mormons. It is without doubt another gospel.

Once again we would point out features in this cult which

[1] Orson Pratt, *Divine Authority of Book of Mormon.*
[2] *Book of Mormon*, Sec. cxxxii, 44.
[3] *Doctrines and Covenants*, p. 248.
[4] *Contributions of Joseph Smith*, p. 7.
[5] *Articles of Faith.*

appear in several others: Writings which rank as of equal authority with the Scriptures; denial of most of the fundamental truths of the Scripture; salvation by works; inconsistency in life of its founders; exclusion of members of all other sects from the number of the elect.

The command of Scripture concerning such is clear: "From such, turn away."

XI

SEVENTH-DAY ADVENTISM

LEADERS of the Seventh-Day Adventist Church published in 1957 an authoritative statement of their beliefs which has clarified many points on which considerable confusion existed in their publications. The book of 700 pages, *Seventh-Day Adventists Answer Questions on Doctrine*, published by the Review and Herald Publishing Association, Washington, D.C., has made necessary a fresh evaluation of the movement. The opening chapter lists nineteen articles of belief held by Adventists in common with the historic Protestant creeds. These include all the doctrines usually considered essential by evangelical Christians. Then follow twelve articles of belief on which alternative views are held by "conservative Christians." Lastly come five areas of thought which are distinctive with Adventists. With these statements before us, we shall endeavour to assess the status of this cult.

It is pertinent to ask if this book does, in fact, express the real and uniform teaching of the Seventh-Day Adventist Church. Does it come with the imprimatur of the Church's supreme authorities? Let the authors speak for themselves. They affirm that the subject matter of the book was "prepared by a group of recognised leaders, in close counsel with Bible teachers, editors and administrators. The goal was to set forth our basic beliefs in terminology currently used in theological circles. This was *not* to be a new statement of faith. It was natural that these answers would come within the framework of the official statement of Fundamental Beliefs of Seventh-Day Adventists which appears in the *Church Manual*. . . . In view of this fact, these answers represent the position of our denomination in the area of church doctrine and prophetic interpretation. . . . The answers in this volume are an expansion of our doctrinal positions contained in the official statement of Fundamental Beliefs already referred to. Hence this volume can be viewed as truly representative of the faith and beliefs of the Seventh-Day Adventist Church."[1]

In this chapter we are accepting *Questions on Doctrine* as the authoritative teaching of the movement. While we are glad to have this clarifying statement, we cannot but feel that more frankness in retracting former statements of doctrine which were equivocal, to say the least, and which have given rise to such grave misgivings among evangelical Christians, would have served to create greater confidence in their bona fides. In considering their present position, it should be borne in mind that it has been the Adventists who have attacked some of the general beliefs of evangelical Christians, and that they have been the aggressors, not we.

ITS FOUNDERS

The real founder of the sect was William Miller, who was converted from sceptical deism in 1816 and later joined a Baptist church. He conceived the idea of laying aside all human writings on the Bible and giving himself to an elaborate study of Bible prophecy. His motive was doubtless good, but the results of his study brought tragedy to many. His research led him to the conclusion that the end of the world would come on October 10, 1843, and he induced many to his way of thinking. When the day passed without the expected return of Christ, the date was advanced to October 22, 1844, but with the same result. He later acknowledged his error and expressed his regret, for he was a godly man.

At this point Miller faded out of the picture and two of his followers, Elder and Mrs. Ellen G. White, formerly Ellen Harmon, came into prominence. It should be stated in fairness to him that Miller repudiated the new theories which later grew out of the movement. Mrs. White was destined to become the prophetess of the movement; her visions and writings are still foundational in Seventh-Day Adventist teaching.

The place she holds in the Church is stated thus: "That the Spirit of prophecy or the prophetic gift is one of the gifts of the Spirit promised to the Church in these last days, and that the gift was manifested to the Seventh-Day Adventist Church

[1] *Questions on Doctrine*, p. 10.

in the work and writings of Ellen G. White."[1] Concerning the degree of authority to be accorded to Mrs. White's writings, they assert : "We do not regard the writings of Ellen G. White as an addition to the sacred canon of Scripture. We do not think of them as of universal application as is the Bible, but particularly for the Seventh-Day Adventist Church. We do not regard them in the same sense as the Holy Scriptures which stand alone and unique as the standard by which all other writings must be judged."[2]

But while Adventists do not place the inspiration of Mrs. White's writings on a level with that of the Scriptures, a perusal of their literature leaves the clear impression that her writings hold a place of authority in the Church which has few equals in contemporary church history. She herself, in referring to one of her pronouncements, said, "It is God, and not an erring mortal who has spoken." This was a most unwise if not dangerous claim to make, especially when a comparison of later editions of Mrs. White's writings with the earlier reveal many changes on every page. Adventists have little grounds for surprise if those who read such statements conclude that their founder claimed a high degree of inspiration for herself. They themselves class her writings as "inspired counsel and instruction."[3]

Mrs. White tells of having suffered a serious injury to her head when a girl, which resulted in fainting and epileptic fits, a condition conducive to seeing visions. Dr. William Russell, a chief physician at the Seventh-Day Adventist sanatorium at Battle Creek, himself long an Adventist, wrote in 1869 that her visions were the result of a diseased organization or condition of the brain or nervous system. Dr. Fairfield, another Adventist, stated in 1897 that he had no doubt that her visions were simply hysterical trances. It was doubtless these visions and other unusual if not startling interpretations and predictions which drew around her a growing group of admirers. She died in 1915 at the age of eighty-eight.

The Church which she founded has made rapid growth, as the statistics given by Walter R. Martin in *Christianity Today* (December 19, 1960, p. 13) reveal. Their 12,500 churches

[1] *Questions on Doctrine*, p. 25.
[2] Ibid., p. 89.
[3] Ibid., p. 92.

have more than 1,155,000 in membership, while Sabbath School members number 1,500,000. There are 6,000 ordained ministers. They operate 44 publishing houses, producing literature in over 200 languages. They publish 385 periodicals and more than 60 new books annually. They have enrolled more than 3,000,000 in their free Bible Study courses. Their "Voice of Prophecy" radio programme is broadcast over 860 stations, and their "Faith for Today" TV programme over 153 stations in U.S.A. alone. These impressive figures indicate a movement with both vision and vitality. In their large missionary programme, they have more than 1,400 workers.

In their activities there has been an element of deception which has caused a great deal of heart-searching among the more conscientious of their own members. It has been their general practice to conceal their identity for as long as possible. The sponsorship of their large meetings has not been disclosed. Their radio broadcasts have not revealed their Adventist associations, nor do they disclose their peculiar and distinctive teachings, but reserve them for subsequent contacts. Their literature does not disclose its origin, and their colporteurs usually reveal their identity only after very straight speaking. Instead, they will affirm they are representing interdenominational missions or give some such evasive answer. That this is by design and not by accident, the writer has learned from Adventists who have deplored the methods adopted.

In his *Answers to Questions*, F. D. Nichol admits that this was in effect official policy, adopted because the "slanderous myths" circulated about the movement would have precluded their getting a hearing. However, he states, "We are increasingly following the plan of announcing at the outset the Adventist sponsorship of the public meetings. That is what we like to do, and what we hope ere long to be able to do everywhere. . . . If in order to secure an initial hearing we must first conceal the name, we do so for a brief period only with a view to a clear-cut announcement of our Adventist connections a little later in our meetings."

We learn that the "Voice of Prophecy" has of recent days revealed its Adventist associations, and for this advance in honesty in public relations we can be grateful. But the publicity for the Twentieth Century Bible Course, so widely advertised over the radio, showed the same tendency to dissimulation. The attractively printed folder advertising the course, which fell into our hands some time ago, gave quotations from Luther, Wesley, Spurgeon and Moody, but with no word to indicate that there was any divergence in teaching between these men and the sponsors of the course. We trust that the tendency to honest identification will extend to all the Church's activities. Readers should know that publications of the *Signs Publishing Company* and *Review and Herald Publishing Association* are of Adventist origin.

We shall now review the doctrines of Seventh-Day Adventism, as set out in *Questions on Doctrine*.

MAJOR FUNDAMENTAL DOCTRINES

In this official statement Adventists affirm without equivocation that they stand with historic evangelical Christianity on these doctrines: The Trinity; the pre-existence and deity of Christ, His Virgin birth and sinless life, His vicarious, atoning death, His bodily resurrection and ascension and triestly ministry and mediation, His premillennial return; the deity and personality of the Holy Spirit; the depravity of man; salvation through Christ by grace alone, through faith in His blood; the entrance upon new life through regeneration; justification by faith; sanctification through the Spirit.

While accepting the assurance that these evangelical doctrines are embraced by the leaders of Seventh-Day Adventism, we must make reference to ambiguous statements of past days which have given justifiable grounds for considering them to be heterodox in doctrine. Some of these questionable statements have now been satisfactorily explained, but others still leave a question in the mind.

The Atonement

Here are some statements which undoubtedly, taken as they stand, have a flavour of heterodoxy:

"The blood of Christ, pleaded in behalf of penitent believers, secured their pardon and acceptance with the Father, yet their sins still remained upon the books of record."[1]

"Christ did not make atonement when He shed His blood upon the cross. Let this fact be fixed for ever in the mind."[2]

"It is impossible to conclude that a complete work of

[1] White, *The Great Controversy.*
[2] Smith, *Looking unto Jesus,* p. 237.

atoning for sin was wrought upon the cross . . . the work of atonement must continue as long as probationary time shall last."[1]

"The blood of Christ, while it was to release the repentant sinner from the condemnation of the law, was not to cancel sin; it would stand on record in the sanctuary until the final payment."[2]

"As in typical service there was a work of atonement at the close of the year, so before Christ's work for redemption of men is completed, there is a work of atonement for the removal of sin from the sanctuary. This is the service which began when the 2,300 days ended" (in 1844).[3]

Such teaching is entirely irreconcilable with such passages as Heb. 1: 3; 9: 11, 12; 10: 12–14.

Adventists claim that these statements of Smith and Watson, who wrote eighty years ago, have since been repudiated by the Church. Over against the above statement of Mrs. White is another quotation from the *Review and Herald*, September 21, 1901, which appears to contradict it. "Christ planted the cross between heaven and earth, and when He beheld the sacrifice of His Son He bowed before it in recognition of His perfection. 'It is enough,' He said. 'The atonement is completed.'" There are thus inconsistencies in her teaching on this subject and in other Adventist publications statements on the subject are far from satisfactory. In explanation of the present stand of the Church on this theme, Adventist leaders write, "When one hears an Adventist say or reads in Adventist literature in the writings of Ellen G. White that Christ is making atonement now, it should be understood that we mean simply that Christ is now making application of the benefits of the sacrificial atonement He made on the cross; that He is making it efficacious for us individually according to our needs and requests."

Actually this is an over-simplification of the matter, for Adventist teaching on the Atonement is linked with their peculiar "Sanctuary teaching." They give a particular turn to the interpretation of Christ's atoning and mediatorial work in what they hold about His present "investigative judgment." This arises directly from the failure of Christ to appear in 1844.

[1] Watson, *The Atoning Work of Christ*, pp. 95, 97.
[2] White, *Patriarchs and Prophets*, p. 357.
[3] White, *The Great Controversy*.

While some held that the calculations were at fault, the Seventh-Day Adventists maintained that 1844 marked Christ's movement to the heavenly sanctuary to cleanse it from sin. This idea is thought to be supported by the pattern of the Day of Atonement in Lev. 16, by Dan. 8: 14 and Heb. 9: 23.

The teaching is difficult to follow, but the idea is that all the deeds of men are recorded in God's books, as are also the names of those who have accepted Christ as Saviour. Since 1844 Christ has been investigating the life-books of every person who has ever lived, and blotting out from the heavenly records the sins of all those who are saved through the blood of Jesus Christ. There is thus a difference between the forgiveness of sins, which the believer experiences now, and the final blotting out of sins from the universe.

Apart from the special interpretation that is given to the type picture in Lev. 16, there is no clear Scripture for a distinction of this kind. It is a strange idea that the blood of Jesus Christ cleanses from all sin, while yet the sin remains written in heaven until the second coming. Scripture says, "Now once at the end of the ages hath he been manifested to put away sin by the sacrifice of himself" (Heb. 9: 26, R.V.).[1]

Satan as Sin-bearer

A statement by Mrs. E. G. White has caused many to believe that she regarded Satan as the bearer of the sin of the believer. Here are the words which gave rise to this belief: "It was seen that while Christ the sin offering pointed to Christ as a sacrifice, and the great high priest represented Christ as Mediator, the Scapegoat typified Satan, the author of sin, upon whom the sins of the truly penitent will be finally placed . . . he will at last suffer the full penalty of sin in the fires that shall destroy all the wicked."[2]

Taken as it stands, this careless statement would convey the impression that Satan bore the sins of the penitent in a vicarious sense. The present leaders, however, have made clear their repudiation of this idea. "Seventh-Day Adventists repudiate in toto any idea, suggestion or implication that Satan is in any sense or degree our sin-bearer. The thought is abhorrent to us and appallingly sacrilegious." "Satan will ultimately

[1] Sanders and Wright, *Some Modern Religions*, pp. 20, 21.
[2] *The Great Controversy*, pp. 419, 422, 485, 486.

have to bear the retributive punishment for his responsibility in the sins of all men, both righteous and wicked."[1] While gladly accepting this assurance, we still believe their interpretation of the scapegoat to be misleading and unscriptural.

The Sinlessness of Christ

Statements have been made by Adventist writers, Mrs. E. G. White among them, which have either affirmed or implied that Christ inherited a sinful nature. One such statement appeared in *Bible Readings for the Home Circle* (1944) which has had a very wide circulation. "In his humanity Christ partook of our sinful, fallen nature. If not, then He was not made like unto His brethren. . . . On the human side Christ inherited just what every child of Adam inherits—a sinful nature." We learn that in 1945 the statement was expunged because it was not in line with official Adventist theology.[2] Elsewhere in her writings Mrs. White said, "We should have no misgivings in regard to the perfect sinlessness of the human nature of Christ."[3]

Human Destiny and the Future State

In the statement of *Fundamental Beliefs* we read: "'God only hath immortality' (1 Tim. 6: 16). Mortal man possesses a nature inherently sinful and dying. Eternal life is the gift of God through faith in Christ (Rom. 6: 23). . . . Immortality is bestowed upon the righteous at the second coming of Christ, when the righteous dead are raised from the grave and the living righteous translated to meet the Lord. Then it is that those accounted faithful 'put on immortality.'"

"The condition of man in death is one of unconsciousness. That all men good and evil alike remain in the grave from death to the resurrection."

"The finally impenitent, including Satan, the author of sin, will, by the fires of the last day be reduced to a state of non-existence, becoming as though they had not been, thus purging God's universe of sin and sinners."[4]

It is of course true that only God has inherent immortality, but this does not prove that the dead "know not anything."

[1] *Questions on Doctrine*, p. 400.
[2] Martin, *Truth About Seventh-Day Adventism*, p. 86.
[3] *Signs of the Times*, June 9, 1898.
[4] *Questions on Doctrine*, p. 14.

If that were so, it would be a new creation, not a resurrection that is necessary. The teaching of Scripture is that at physical birth man becomes possessed of *endless being*; at his new birth he receives *eternal life*; at the resurrection he receives an *incorruptible* and *immortal* body. Immortality in its strict sense refers only to that which takes place at the resurrection when the believer who once inhabited a mortal and corruptible body puts on a body incorruptible (exempt from decay) and immortal (exempt from death). In Rom. 2: 7 and 2 Tim. 1: 10 the word "immortality" should be rendered "incorruptible."

As to the theory of soul-sleep, our Lord and the apostles consistently referred to eternal life as being bestowed the moment one exercised faith in Christ (John 6: 47; 10: 28; 17: 23). Being life there must be consciousness, and being eternal, there cannot be interruption in its continuity.

For answer concerning annihilation see Matt. 10: 28; 25: 46; Mark 3: 29; Luke 12: 4, 5; 16: 19–31; Rev. 20: 10–15.

Justification by Faith

Another generally held view is that their legalism and insistence on sabbath observance neutralises their claim that salvation is through faith alone. These statements would confirm this view:

"Those who accept the Saviour, however sincere their conversion, should never be taught to say or feel that they are saved. This is misleading."[1]

"Jesus has purchased redemption for us. It is ours but we are placed on probation to see if we will prove worthy of eternal life."[2]

"The condition of eternal life is now just what it always has been . . . perfect obedience to the law of God."[3]

Adventists believe that a believer can fall away and be lost, a doctrine which is unacceptable to most evangelical Christians. While they profess to have embraced the best of both Calvinism and Arminianism, basically they are Arminian in emphasis, and this emphasis in many of their writings conveys the idea that salvation depends on legal observance.

[1] *Christ's Object Lessons*, p. 155.
[2] *Testimonies for the Church*, Vol. I, p. 199.
[3] *Steps to Christ*, pp. 65, 67.

True they claim, "According to Seventh-Day Adventist belief, there is and can be no salvation through the law, or by human works of the law, but only through the saving grace of God." But logically their teaching concerning the sabbath is a negation of this claim.

Sabbath Observance

This is a seventh-day cult, and its attitude to Sunday observance is of fundamental importance in assessing its merits or dangers.

"The sign or seal of God is revealed in the observance of the seventh-day sabbath, the Lord's memorial of creation . . . the mark of the beast is the opposite of this—the observance of the first day of the week."[1] As the mark of the beast involves its recipients being "tormented with fire and brimstone . . . for ever and ever" (Rev. 14: 9–11), this is a terrifying prospect and could have a devastating effect on a sensitive mind.

However such a statement is explained—and Adventists do explain it by quoting another passage from Mrs. White—it is sufficiently equivocal to have caused great concern to many. Such warnings have bound many to the movement through legalistic fear, and induced others to join it for the same reason. The author has seen intelligent Adventists literally trembling and weeping in fear of the woes that would fall on them if they seceded. And these fears arose from the writings of Mrs. White.

The statement of Mrs. White which is advanced to refute the above idea is: "Sunday keeping is not yet the mark of the beast, and will not be until the decree goes forth causing men to worship this idol sabbath. The time will come when this day will be the test, but that test has not come yet."[2]

Lord's Day or Sabbath

Adventists believe that the keeping of the sabbath, commanded in the decalogue, is binding on all men for all time. They assert that the churches have changed a seventh-day sabbath into a first-day sabbath, and in their teaching there is a strong implication that sabbath keeping is essential to salvation. The Scripture teaches not that "the Jewish sabbath

[1] *Testimonies for the Church*, Vol. VIII, p. 117.
[2] Ellen G. White, Manuscript 118, 1899.

132

is to be changed, but that in fulfilment of prophecy it has been in this dispensation, made 'to cease,' for, said God through Hosea, 'I will cause her (Israel's) mirth to cease, her feasts, her new moons, her sabbaths, and all her solemn assemblies' (Hos. 2: 11), this being in consequence of the nation having become for the time being, *lo ammi*, i.e. in God's sight 'not my people' (Hos. 1: 9). Nor is there any 'first-day sabbath.' The Christian's day of worship is the Lord's Day."[1]

The following reasons are advanced for rejecting these Adventist claims:

1. Sabbath keeping was enjoined only on Israel, to whom alone it was given as a sign from God (Exod. 31: 13, 17), and as a memorial of their Egyptian bondage and God's deliverance (Deut. 5: 12–15).

2. The Lord's Day of the Christian at once upholds the abiding principles of rest and worship for which the Jewish sabbath was instituted, and is a remembrance of His resurrection from the dead on the first day of the week.

3. Read in its context (Exod. 19–24), the decalogue is seen to be inseparably connected with the Sinaitic or Old Covenant, while we are now under the New Covenant of grace. See Rom. 6: 14, 15; 10: 4–9; 2 Cor. 3: 7–11; Gal. 3: 24–25; 4: 1–7; 5: 13, 14; Heb. 8: 9, 13.

4. In the New Testament each commandment of the decalogue is reiterated and greatly expanded in its application *except the fourth* relating to the sabbath, which is nowhere mentioned. See Rom. 14: 1–7; Gal. 4: 10, 11: Col. 2: 14–17. Why this significant omission if it is of such commanding importance? Every important subject has extended treatment somewhere in the New Testament. Why not this one? In the various lists of sins, nowhere is failure to observe the sabbath specified.

5. Scripture expressly declares that sabbath-keeping is not obligatory on the Christian. "Let no man therefore judge you in meat, or in drink, or in respect of an holy day, or of the new moon, or of the sabbath days (a sabbath day R.V.); *which are a shadow* of things to come" (Col. 2: 16, 17). Adventists regard this reference as applying to the extra ceremonial sabbaths and not the weekly sabbath.[2] But it would be impossible for a Jew to use the term "sabbaths" by itself

---
[1] N. C. Deck, *Lord's Day or Sabbath*, p. 10.
[2] *Questions on Doctrine*, p. 159.

if he intended to exclude the weekly sabbath. None of the letters to Gentile Christians contains any reference to the sabbath, except to say that it is abolished.[1]

6. In reality, instead of resulting in salvation the keeping of the sabbath results in its keeper coming under a curse. c.f. Num. 15: 32-36 with Gal. 3: 10.

7. The Council at Jerusalem refused to impose any legal observance upon Gentile believers other than abstinence from food offered to idols, things strangled, and blood (Acts 25: 28, 29).

8. The observance of "days and months and times and years" was denounced by Paul as a legalism which is alien to the Gospel (Gal 4: 10, 11).

In one of her visions Mrs. White records, "I saw that God had not changed the sabbath, but a pope had changed it from the seventh day to the first day, for he was to change times and laws." But this is incapable of substantiation. Actually there was no Pope of Rome at the time the day was supposed to have been changed. A recent leaflet circulated by the "Voice of Prophecy" radio programme aims to prove that Sunday usurped the sabbath and is a pagan institution imposed by Constantine in 321. Others attribute the change to the Council of Laodicea which convened in A.D. 364 and which incidentally was in no sense a Roman Catholic one.

What is the testimony of the Early Church Fathers concerning the observance of the first day of the week?

The Didache or Teaching of the Apostles (A.D. 70-5): "On the Lord's own day, gather yourselves together and break bread and give thanks."

Barnabas (about A.D. 74): "Wherefore we keep the Lord's day with joyfulness, the day also on which Jesus rose from the dead."

Ignatius (A.D. 110): "If then those who walked in the ancient practises, no longer observing sabbaths, but fashioning their lives after the Lord's day on which our life also rose through Him. . . ."

Justin Martyr (A.D. 138): "On the day called Sunday there is a gathering in one place . . . and the memoirs of the apostles and the writings of the prophets are studied."

Irenaeus (A.D. 178): "The mystery of the Lord's resurrection may not be celebrated on any other day than the Lord's day."

[1] Sanders and Wright, *Some Modern Religions*, p. 24.

Clement (A.D. 194): "The old sabbath day has become no more than a working day."

Such testimony could be multiplied, but the foregoing quotations are sufficient to establish that two centuries before the time Adventists suggest the change took place, the Lord's day had become the recognised day of worship for the Early Church. It is regrettable that Adventists, in their attempt to bolster their peculiar tenets, ignore and pervert the testimony both of history and of Scripture on this subject.

Reasons for Observing the First Day

We observe the Lord's day, the first day of the week, not because we must, but because we may; out of love for Him and not from legal constraint.

It was on the first day that Jesus rose from the dead (John 20: 1).

It was foreshadowed in the Feast of Firstfruits (Lev. 23: 15–16), a festival which typified the resurrection of the Lord, which was followed after fifty days by the Feast of Pentecost, typical of the descent of the Holy Spirit.

It was on the first day that Jesus met His people after His resurrection (Luke 24: 13–31; John 20: 19). Again a week later He met with them (John 20: 26). Thus the Lord's day was born.

It was on the first day that the Holy Spirit descended to constitute the New Testament Church.

It was on the first day that the rite of Christian baptism was first observed (Acts 2: 41).

It was on the first day that the New Testament Church met for worship (Acts 20: 7; Rev. 1: 10).

It was on the first day believers were exhorted to make their offerings (1 Cor. 16: 2).

It was on the first day that Christians met to observe the Lord's Supper which had superseded the Passover Feast.

In conclusion, in view of their claims that keepers of the sabbath have "the seal of God," while observers of the Lord's Day will in a coming day, if not today, have "the mark of the beast," it would be justifiable to ask Adventists some questions concerning their own sabbath-keeping:

Since the observance of the sabbath is an unchangeable law, do they keep the whole law of the sabbath strictly themselves? Do they keep the other sabbaths of Israel? Do they stone any who gather sticks on the sabbath? Do they observe circumcision which is the other sign of the divine covenant with them? If not, does not the curse rather than the blessing of God rest on them?

Let us praise God for the liberty of the Gospel, and resting on Rom. 14: 4–6 and Col. 2: 16, let us refuse to allow anyone to replace on our shoulders a yoke of bondage from which the cross of Christ has for ever delivered us.

XII

BRITISH-ISRAELISM

WHILE it would be both untrue and unfair to place British-Israelism in the same category as Christian Science and Spiritism, it is nevertheless true that in many cases it effectively sidetracks those who embrace it. Spiritism is anti-Christian, British-Israelism, extra-Christian. It is nationalistic rather than Christo-centric. We hasten to add that many convinced adherents of this theory are loyal evangelicals who would never think of denying any fundamental truth of the faith, and for this reason what follows is entirely without rancour, and has reference to the theory rather than to those who embrace it.

One of its most able opponents, Rev. Samuel H. Wilkinson of the Mildmay Mission to the Jews, in his examination of the claims of British-Israelism, conceded that "It has developed a considerable literature, some of it is very able; and has indeed established a very plausible prima facie case which deserves and demands examination."

"British-Israelism is not capable of argument," said the charitable Dr. F. B. Meyer, "it is a kind of infatuation." And argument is useless with one who is infatuated. There are some theories which are so palpably astray, that argument is at once impossible and unnecessary. When the verdict of scholarship and history and the voice of large tracts of Scripture are ignored, no common basis for argument exists. We shall, therefore, endeavour to present positive evidence that this is done in British-Israelism, and leave it to the reader to draw his own conclusions.

ORIGIN AND GROWTH

The origin of British-Israelism is variously ascribed to the French Magistrate, Counsellor Le Loyer, who wrote, *The Ten Lost Tribes Found*, in 1590; to Dr. Abbadie of Amsterdam who wrote in 1723, "The ten tribes must be sought for in the North and West and in the British Isles"; to Richard

Brothers, who in 1822 published a book, *The Invasion of England by the Saxons*.

Towards the end of last century its ablest apologists were Edward Hine and John Wilson, to whom much of the popularity and growth of the movement must be attributed. Later, C. Piazzi Smyth, Astronomer-Royal for Scotland, linked the pyramid measurements to the British-Israel theory, thus confusing the issue, and still further justifying Dr. Meyer's remark quoted above. The Rev. Pascoe Goard's gracious personality and able presentation of his case was a strength to the movement. The adoption of the belief by Pentecostal groups has also secured for it many ardent adherents.

Principal Tenets

In brief, the main teachings of the movement are these:

The lost ten tribes have reappeared in the English-speaking peoples.

The reigning British monarch is a true descendant of King David.

The promises to Israel are being or will be fulfilled nationally in the English-speaking peoples.

There is a vital distinction in Scripture between Israel and the Jews, each having a different destiny. The word "Jew" refers to Judah and Benjamin alone, while "Israel" refers to the Ten Tribes.

Dr. J. J. Mountain, one of the ablest apologists of the movement, expressed it thus: "We Anglo-Saxons are the lineal descendants of the Ten Tribes, we are the national posterity of Israel, and we inherit the wonderful promises made to them. These promises we possess nationally. But we can become individually Israel's spiritual posterity only by being born again." If it were suggested that to the English-speaking nations had been entrusted the spiritual heritage which in olden times was the sacred trust of Israel, we could see much to support such a view, but with reference to the nationalistic claims of British-Israelites, we will find no supporting evidence. On the contrary, we submit that:

Scholastically, *it is Discredited*

The court of secular scholarship is the last to which the believer would appeal for a decision on purely spiritual truth, for spiritual things are only spiritually discerned. But this theory is concerned rather with history, ethnology, philology, and anthropology, all of which can be tested by secular scholarship. And what is the verdict of competent scholars?

Professor R. W. Chambers, M.A., D.Litt., who holds the chair of the English Language in the London University, replied to a letter from Mr. George Goodman in the following terms:

"I do not believe that there is any reason for regarding the West Germanic peoples as descendants of the Tribes of Israel which were scattered from Palestine during the early captivities.

1. The racial characteristics are quite different. The present-day Jew is typically different from the Englishman, Dutchman or German. If he resembles them, it is generally because he is not of pure Jewish descent.

2. There is no trace of Judaism in Germanic folk lore.

3. The Germanic languages are absolutely distinct from the Semitic.

4. So are the old Germanic laws."

The Encyclopædia Britannica, in an article on the subject states, "The theory of Anglo-Israelism rests on premises which are deemed by scholars, both theological and anthropological to be utterly unsound."

Chambers's Encyclopædia characterises it as "A theory that sets at defiance all ethnological and linguistic evidence."

To all but those already committed to the theory, such weighty and impartial statements should certainly give pause.

FACTUALLY, *it is erroneous*

Tested by fact, British-Israelism makes a poor showing.

In the realm of *philology*, there is no more affinity between English and Hebrew than there is between English and Chinese.

As to *physiognomy*, there is strong contrast rather than striking similarity between the large-boned, fair-haired, blue-eyed Briton and the thick-set, swarthy, brown-eyed Israelite.

In the matter of *graphology*, Israel has always written from right to left, while the Anglo-Saxons have always written from left to right. Such a radical change would be impossible except by direct compulsion, but evidence of such a change is totally lacking.

Racially, the British and Americans even more so, are extraordinarily mixed. Unlike the Hebrews, they have freely intermingled with other races, and to a large extent racial identity has been lost. Unlike the Hebrews, too, they are uncircumcised, and have therefore forfeited any claim to blessing under the covenant (Gen. 17: 14; Gal. 6: 15).

Of Israel it was said, "Israel shall abide many days without a King" (Hos. 3: 4, 5). Is this true of Britain?

"The people shall dwell alone, and shall not be reckoned among the nations," prophesied Balaam under divine compulsion (Num. 23: 9). Is this fulfilled in Britain?

"They shall be wanderers among the nations" (Hos. 9: 17). Is this characteristic of Britain?

British-Israelites claim, again in the words of Dr. J. J. Mountain, that "the Anglo-Saxon race have come under the New Covenant by the acceptance of Christian faith." Unfortunately, this is not a fact. Nationally, it would be far more true to say that we have rejected the Christian faith, if current statistics mean anything.

"It is a tremendous strain on the doctrine of election," says Rev. J. A. McMillan, "to imagine that, out of the hordes of Jutes, Saxons, Danes, Norsemen, and later Norman-French, those only who came into the British Isles and maintained there their footing by right of conquest, were the descendants of the roving ten tribes, and that others of the above-named races who did not come into Britain were not Israelites. It is hard to accept the theory that of the masses who invaded various parts of Europe, a certain elect group were kept separate from the rest as a people of God, to be made manifest in a land of His choosing."

HISTORICALLY, *it is Unsubstantiated*

The theory is thoroughly untenable on historical grounds. So far as we are aware, no competent and reputable historian has identified himself with the movement. Some of the "missing links" in genealogical tables in support of British-Israelism which we have perused, would utterly discredit any historian who sponsored it.

Let us examine some of their historic claims.

1. *The Ten Tribes were lost, and have reappeared in the British and American nations*. We submit that there is not a scintilla of evidence in either sacred or profane history to substantiate this claim, but there is very much to the contrary.

The main point at issue centres around the whereabouts and identification of the ten tribes, who were carried off into captivity. British-Israelites assert that the British people are the descendants of the ten-tribed kingdom which was deported to Assyria, and thence migrated westward to the British Isles and America. Let us examine this contention.

"The captivity" was not an event, but a long series of events extending over 150 years, from 730 B.C. under Tiglath-Pileser (2 Kings 15: 29) until 586 B.C. under Nebuchadnezzar (Jer. 52: 28–30). Between these dates, several deportations were made, the numbers being approximately as follows:

Tiglath-Pileser	.	.	.	200,000
Sargon	.	.	.	27,290
Sennacherib	.	.	.	200,150
Nebuchadnezzar	.	.	.	100,000

By the latter date, the Jewish community in Assyria must have been approaching 2,000,000. At any rate they were so numerous that Petronius, Roman Legate of Syria, deemed it dangerous to excite in them a hostile disposition towards Rome.

Recent research has however established the fact that the Israel of the captivity included, not only those from the ten tribes, but also many exiles from Judah and Benjamin. During the two hundred years from the first deportation, these groups had become so thoroughly amalgamated that they were never again separated.

Just as the captivity extended over a long period, so did the return from exile. Under Zerubbabel and Ezra, we gather from the record that probably more than 150,000 returned to Palestine and settled in Judea. In addition to these, there were doubtless unrecorded migrations to the land, of exiles who had settled in Galilee and Samaria, which had been depopulated by Tiglath-Pileser. That they were free thus to return, is clear from the inscription by Cyrus which showed this to be his settled policy for all his dominions.

The initiative in the return is ascribed to the men of Judah and Benjamin, but this is easily understandable, for they were the most recent captives in whom national consciousness would be most clear and strong. As Dr. A. Pieters points out, the ordinary term by which the people are designated, is not

"Judah," or "the Jews," but "Israel." In Ezra, "Judah" occurs five times, "the Jews" seven times, "Israel" forty-one times—surely a satisfactory indication that the ancient breach between Israel and Judah had been healed. The sacrifices offered were "twelve he-goats according to the number of the tribes of Israel" (Ezra 6: 17).

Ezekiel employs the phrase, "the whole house of Israel," to make it clear that the whole ten tribes as one re-united nation, were intended (37: 11; 39: 25; 45: 6). In Daniel, Haggai, Zechariah and Malachi, "Israel" is sometimes placed in contrast to Judah (e.g. Dan. 9: 7), sometimes refers to men of Judah (e.g. Dan. 1: 3), sometimes includes both Israel and Judah (e.g. Dan. 9: 20).

In the book of Esther, there is no other name for the exiles than "the Jews," who scattered from India to Ethiopia. From their number, distribution and influence, it is clear that all Israelites are referred to. Those to whom the execution of the decree for the extermination of the Jews was entrusted, would certainly have a problem on their hands to distinguish between those descended from the ten tribes and those descended from Judah and Benjamin!

The clear and reasonable inference thus is, that the later prophets and writers increasingly ignored any distinction between Israel and Judah, but used both terms for the re-united people. The New Testament record agrees with this position. There is no reference anywhere to the ten tribes as a separate group. On the contrary, see Matt. 19: 28; Acts 26: 7; Jas. 1: 1.

In order to identify Britain with Israel, it is essential to the British-Israel scheme to identify with the Scythians, the ten lost tribes, and the Norsemen with the Scythians, and the British with the Norsemen. S. H. Wilkinson has stated the argument thus: The ten tribes are stated in the Apocrypha to have migrated to Asareth, which must have been the river and town of Sareth in the Carpathians. The Scythians were in the same district at the same time, therefore the two are identical. Sharon Turner has suggested that the Saxons were migrants into N.W. Europe from the Asiatic side of the Araxes. Paul du Chaillu sets out a "fairly continuous history" which represents the progenitors of the English-speaking people as having migrated from the shores of the Black Sea. Therefore the Scythians were Israel, the Norsemen were the

Scythians, the British Empire was peopled from Scandinavia
and—the British are Israel. Such a tenuous claim, surely
requires a firmer foundation than their unhistorical assertions
afford.

2. *The Throne of Britain is the Throne of David*, and the
reigning British monarch is a true descendant of David.

The assertion is that Jeremiah brought away the elder
daughter of Zedekiah, last King of Judah, Tea-Tephi by name,
first to Spain and then to Ireland, where in 580 B.C. she
married a tribal chief. From then till A.D. 404 the line of
David was continued there, and then transferred to the Kings
of Argyleshire, and later to the Kings of Scotland, and later
still to James I. Then, through a king of Bohemia and a
princess of Brunswick to George I and thence to Queen
Elizabeth II!

Scripture, however, explicitly teaches that Israel's King is
to sit on David's throne *in Jerusalem* (Isa. 9: 7; Jer. 3: 17;
Ezek. 48: 35). But even if the assertion were true, it would
create as many difficulties as it solved, for the royal tribe
was Judah, not one of the ten tribes, and our Queen would
thus be disqualified.

Further, as the oldest Irish manuscript belongs to the
tenth century A.D., and letters were not used there earlier
than the fifth century A.D., how could her pedigree be traced
through various families, and in various countries? In this
way, our British-Israelite friends, while claiming to be Ephraim,
appropriate to themselves Judah's King and throne.

To us the final appeal is to the Scriptures, and not to
fallible volumes of ancient history and genealogical trees.

3. *The Great Pyramid has a prophetic voice*, and this voice
corroborates their claim. We will not embarrass our friends
by recalling the many unfulfilled predictions which have been
based on the interior measurements of the pyramid. We will
be content to state that the pyramid was simply a pagan
Egyptian tomb, with no more spiritual significance than any
of the other burial places of the Kings.

Sir W. Flinders Petrie who carefully measured the whole
of the interior of the Great Pyramid, tells in his *Seventy Years
in Archaeology* how he found one of the pyramid "prophets"
busily filing away part of the interior of the pyramid to
make the pyramid fit his theory about it!

The claim is based on Isa. 19: 18–21, to which please refer.

But an altar, to comply with divinely given precepts, must not be constructed of hewn stones (Exod. 20 : 25–26). The pyramid breaks this precept. It is neither a "pillar" nor an "altar." These facts alone will be sufficient to convince anyone with an unprejudiced mind that this is merely another unfounded human speculation.

4. Language, physiognomy, customs

This aspect of the subject has already been touched on, but we give the words of the late Rev. Joseph W. Kemp:

"We are asked to believe, forsooth, that nearly three million Israelites poured into Britain, and that they dropped their language, physiognomy, customs, records, their names and their memory; and what is equally astonishing, that for two thousand years nobody seems to have suspected the astounding fact. The thing, of course, never occurred, and I doubt if in the whole world there could be found a historian of any note who would risk his reputation by averring it did. Synagogues and customs (circumcision, for instance) mark today every city to which the Jew has wandered. Further, that an entire race, which once wrote from right to left should, without leaving a single trace of the process behind, revolutionize its penmanship by now writing from left to right, is impossible to conceive."

That there are striking superficial resemblances between the position of Britain in the world today, and that which is prophesied of Israel, we do not deny. But such similarities existed, in measure, in Rome and Greece. Only by ignoring such prophecies as Rom. 11 : 19–35 and Hos. 1 : 4–6 and many others can such resemblances be taken as proof of the theory. There are Japanese who have promulgated a Japanese-Israel theory using similar arguments.

Spiritually, *it is Sterile*

As has been suggested, the main appeal of British-Israelism is to national pride rather than to spirituality. We are not for a moment inferring that all adherents of British-Israelism are unspiritual, but it is quite possible to be a good British-Israelite without any experience of the new birth. It is not *essentially* Christian, and can cohabit happily with a denial of the fundamental truths of the faith, while drawing much of its appeal from its pseudo-religious background. We appreciate the fact that some sections of the movement carefully safeguard their membership.

With few exceptions, British-Israelites become more zealous in obtaining converts to their theory than in winning converts to Christ. Many who were much used of God become mere shadows of their former spiritual selves. There is little life-changing evangelism among them, their lectures being largely on the level of the human intellect. They have little to their credit in the way of missionary interest and achievement, even among the large Jewish populations of the world. Even the incentive provided by their belief in the Second Advent of Christ appears to have little effect in stimulating them to aggression in their soul-winning endeavours.

XIII

FREEMASONRY

"I CONSIDER what is called 'the work' of the Masonic lodge to be childish and foolish. I once took time to study 'the work' of the lodges up to the Royal Arch degree. At that time I knew exactly what they did, and I could never understand how a serious-minded man could give time to such tomfoolery. I could understand a child's doing it. When I hear Masons talking together about 'the work' of the lodge, I can scarcely refrain from laughing. It is difficult for me to see how any man who has a proper amount of self-respect and manly dignity, can go through what a man goes through when he becomes a Master Mason and then ever go back to the lodge again to take part in the initiation of another candidate. To my mind, it is belittling, degrading and disgusting. My attention was called to it when I was about twenty-two years of age, by a man who had been initiated at the Masonic lodge, but came out completely disgusted with his experience and who never went back to the lodge again. How any Christian minister can submit to what a minister is compelled to submit to when he is initiated into the Blue Lodge, I cannot understand. I do not question that there are many excellent men who are members of Masonic lodges, but to me it is incomprehensible how any Christian man can be."

So wrote a world authority whose wide experience and great talents entitled him to speak with an authoritative voice, Dr. Reuben A. Torrey. His verdict is that Freemasonry is futile, and unworthy of the allegiance of grown men. But let us not condemn the Society unheard.

Its Antiquity

In his book,[1] J. S. M. Ward, himself a Mason, claims that the Masonic Order is the oldest religious system in the world and the custodian of the basic ideas common to all religions.

[1] *Freemasonry and the Ancient Gods,*

He traces its origin from the secret societies of antiquity through the ages, to the present orders. Since its rules, symbols and rites are much the same as the ancient mysteries of paganism, there is little doubt as to its heathenish source. Some of the degrees in Masonry are supposed to be a continuation of orders which date back to the Crusades.

The Encyclopædia Britannica, however, maintains that Freemasonry had its rise not earlier than A.D. 1717. Today it boasts almost three million members throughout the world, but not all of these are active members. Its thirty-three degrees, through each of which a Mason must pass before he attains the secrets of the Mystic Shrine, are in three sections:

The Blue Lodge with its three degrees which must be taken before further progress can be made.

The York Rite with its ten degrees, entitling the one who has taken them to membership in the Mystic Shrine. This rite is exclusively for (professing) Christians.

The Scottish Rite, consisting of degrees four to thirty-two which entitle to the honorary thirty-third degree, the Mystic Shrine. This rite is for Jews, Gentiles and Mohammedans.

Its Attractions

No movement draws millions of men into its membership without some very real benefits to offer. What are the special attractions afforded by the Masonic Order?

There is first of all the *social fellowship* for which the hearts of all men crave. Man is essentially a social animal. Many find in the gatherings of their lodge the satisfaction for their social instincts, although in some cases time is spent in the lodge which had better been spent within the family circle. Then, too, there are *commercial advantages* which accrue to the members of the fraternity. The loyalty of a Mason to his fellows in the matter of business preference is proverbial. No small proportion of members of the Order have had their eye more on the material benefits to be derived than on the mastery of its mysteries. Tragically enough, it appears that Christian ministers are attracted to the Order by the supposed *religious advancement* it would secure them. History has proved that too often this step has resulted rather in spiritual impoverishment.

Charles G. Finney, the greatest evangelist of the first half of the last century, himself an ex-Mason, in writing against the Freemasonry he had renounced said: "The fact is that Freemasonry is the most anomalous, absurd and abominable institution that can exist in a Christian country; and is on the face of it, from the fact that it will not allow its principles to be discussed and divulged, a most dangerous thing in human society."

There are not a few Masons who are sensitive about and a little ashamed of the rites of initiation into the Order. From a book[1] which enshrines many Masonic secrets, we learn that when the candidate is initiated in the first degree, his own clothing is removed and he is thinly clad in the clothes provided for him. Next he kneels blindfolded before the Masonic altar, with a light rope around his neck. Arranged on the altar are an open Bible on which rests a square and compass. On either side lighted candles are burning. He is then asked by the Worshipful Master to repeat after him the first Masonic oath, after which the covering is removed from his eyes—and he has entered into the light of Masonry!

Dr. A. C. Dixon, noted Pastor of the Moody Church of Chicago, indicated his reaction to this initiation ceremony. "I would be ashamed to describe the initiation. I felt I had lost some of my influence by submitting to the indignities of that initiation—such as boys would go through and laugh over, but when men come down to them, they are certainly indignities, if not insults." Some readers will find it difficult to believe that intelligent Christians could submit to this foolish and humiliating ceremony, and take on their lips the horrible oaths to which reference is made later.

Nor is this initiation an empty performance to the true Mason. It has a religious significance. Hear the words of A. G. Mackey, Past General High Priest of the General Grand Chapter of the United States, in this connection: "The shock of entrance is, then, the symbol of the disruption of the candidate from the ties of the world, and his introduction into the life of Masonry. It is the symbol of the agonies of death and the throes of the new birth."[2]

---

[1] *King Solomon and His Followers,* No. 13.
[2] *Mackey's Masonic Ritualist,* p. 24.

The state of the initiate prior to the ceremony is described in the same book, pp. 22, 23: "There he stands without our portals, on the threshold of this new Masonic life, in darkness, helplessness and ignorance. Having been wandering amid the errors and covered over with the pollutions of the outer and profane world, he comes inquiring to our doors, seeking the new birth, and asking a withdrawal of the vail which conceals divine truth from his uninitiated sight. . . . There is to be, not simply a change for the future, but also an extinction of the past; for the initiation is, as it were, a death to the world and a resurrection to new life."

But is Masonry the source of the Christian's liberation from the past, his new birth, his death to the world and resurrection to new life?

ITS ABOMINATIONS

Admittedly that is a strong word to use, but we submit that it is no more strong than the case deserves, whether we consider it from the national, ethical or spiritual viewpoint.

Think first of *its blood-curdling oaths*, for every Freemason must take oaths involving penalties which increase in intensity as the degrees advance. In his book,[1] James Putt quoting from *King Solomon and His Followers*, No. 13, gives the oath which is taken by every Mason, as any honest member will admit.

"Of my own free will and accord, in the presence of Almighty God and this worshipful lodge, erected to Him and dedicated to the Holy Saint John, do hereby and hereon, most solemnly and sincerely promise and swear, that I will always hail, forever conceal and never reveal, any of the secret arts, parts, or points of the hidden mysteries of Masonry which may have been heretofore or shall be at this time, or at any future time, communicated to me as such, to any person or persons whatsoever, except it be a true and lawful brother Mason, or within the body of a just and lawfully constituted lodge of Masons; nor unto him or them, until by strict trial, due examination, or lawful information, I shall have found him or them as lawfully entitled to them as I am myself.

"I furthermore promise and swear, that I will not write, print, paint, stamp, stain, cut, carve, hue, make or engrave

[1] *Freemasonry*, p. 26.

them on anything, movable or immovable, capable of receiving the least impression of a sign, word syllable, letter or character whereby they might become legible or intelligible, to any person under the canopy of heaven, and the secrets of Masonry be thus unlawfully obtained by my unworthiness.

"All this I most solemnly and sincerely promise and swear, with a firm and steadfast resolution to keep and perform the same, without the least equivocation, mental reservation, or self-evasion whatsoever, binding myself under no less penalty than that of having my throat cut from ear to ear, my tongue torn out by its roots and buried in the sands of the sea, at low water mark, where the tide ebbs and flows twice in twenty-four hours, should I in the least, knowingly or wittingly, violate or transgress this my Entered Apprentice obligation. So help me God and keep me steadfast."

One Mason, on being faced with the serious implications of the oath, replied, "That doesn't mean anything. Of course, we go through the form, but it doesn't mean anything." Oaths taken on the Bible mean nothing! If they mean nothing, then it is blasphemy to swear them in the name of God. If they mean something and are to be taken seriously and literally, how can a Christian man take such oaths upon himself? Could such oaths ever be justifiable, even apart from the Scriptures which specifically forbid it? See Matt. 5: 14–16, 33–37; Jas. 5: 12.

Then consider *its sworn secrecy*. It is essentially a secret society—secret signs, secret codes, secret meetings. Its oaths are with a view to compelling absolute secrecy on its members. But why must it be secret? Has Masonry something to hide? If not, its secrecy is illogical and unnecessary. If so, then no self-respecting man, not to say no Christian, should join it. Secrecy is opposed to the whole spirit of Christianity, whose benefits are extended not to a few favoured initiates, but to a whole world. Its secrecy panders to the "caste" spirit which is so alien to the ideal of the Christian life. Concealment finds no place in the Christian message. If we have something which is for the good of humanity, it is for us to broadcast it, not to conceal it. Conversely, we should not keep secret any bad thing which should be revealed.

Lastly, ponder the implications of these *oaths of secrecy*. The Masonic bond has been used on many occasions to protect wrongdoers and even major criminals from the just reward of their ill-deeds. The Mason promises and swears "that I will keep the secrets of a companion . . . sacred and inviolable." Can it ever be right to swear and promise beforehand and in ignorance to maintain secrecy concerning events which might prove to be morally and ethically wrong? See Lev. 5: 4, 5. One of the oaths taken involves all Masons in standing by each other in everything, *murder and treason excepted*. But in a higher degree, the oath is with *murder and treason* NOT *excepted*. Such oaths are ethically unjustifiable and judicially culpable. Dr. Torrey testified that in one city where he lived, the proprietor of the vilest and most notorious place in the city could not be touched by the law because he was a Knight Templar. Every other place of the sort was run out of the city. From the purely civic point of view, this element of Masonry is an abomination, and the Christian Mason is liable to become partaker of other men's sins.

ITS ANTICHRISTIANITY

Freemasonry is incompatible with Christianity. Mackey claims that its symbols and rites are antecedent to Christianity, and says, "If Masonry were simply a Christian institution, the Jew and the Moslem, the Brahmin and the Buddhist could not conscientiously partake of its illumination. But its universality is its boast. In its language citizens of every nation may converse; at its altar men of all religions may kneel; to its creed disciples of every faith may subscribe."[1]

Major Powell writes[2]: "Christian saint, Mohammedan mystic, Indian yogi, Buddhist lama, Greek gnostic, Egyptian priest—each in his own way has borne witness to the transcendental vision, where self and personality are obliterated . . . where atonement is established." On p. 105 of the same book appears the blatant autosoterism of Freemasonry: "Before the soul rises again in its glory, there must be Gethsemane and Calvary. There is a loneliness, a desolation of bitterest intensity ere the soul . . . can be itself, *unaided by anything or any being outside itself*, alone, aloof, a King in its own right."

While Freemasonry pays lip-service to a god, it is not the God of the Bible, nor does it give to the Bible a place of pre-

[1] *An Encyclopedia of Freemasonry*, p. 162.
[2] *The Magic of Freemasonry*, p. 194.

eminence over the Koran or the Vedas. God is patronisingly acknowledged as "The Great Architect of the Universe," but W. Hoste asserts that the God of Masonry is "a composite deity—Jehovah, Baal, and On, or Osiris rolled into one, under the initials J.B.O. Novitiates are kept in ignorance of this; they hear the descriptive title, 'the Divine Architect,' and imagine that it is the God of the Bible who is meant. Whereas if Freemasonry be true, the very idol that Jezebel set up in defiance of Jehovah, and On—one of the gods of Egypt against whom Jehovah 'executed judgment'—share the Godhead with Him." See Exod. 20 : 3 ; Isa. 62 : 8.

It is a well-known fact that at least in the lower degrees, the name of Christ is strictly excluded. When clergymen are called on to lead the religious exercises of the lodge, they are frequently instructed not to use the name of Jesus in their prayers, lest a Mohammedan or a Jew be offended. In certain portions of the ritual where New Testament Scriptures are used, the name of Christ is deliberately excised; e.g., the words "by Jesus Christ" are omitted from 1 Pet. 2 : 5. When 2 Thess. 3 : 6 is quoted, the words, "in the name of our Lord Jesus Christ" are omitted, while the words "by our Lord Jesus Christ" do not appear in the quotation from 2 Thess. 3 : 12. It may be true that in some Masonic Lodges the name of Christ is not always excluded, but that is due to the laxity of its officers in enforcing the rulings of the Society.

An ex-Rabbi, Max Wertheimer tells his experience in the following words: "Before I entered the lodge I was told that I would not be required to believe in Jesus Christ as my Saviour or Lord, for that was my objection to joining it as a conscientious, unregenerated Jewish Rabbi! I entered it and became in a short-time Chaplain of the Mystic Lodge (Dayton, Ohio) as a Master Mason. When the Holy Spirit regenerated me, He also convicted me of my sin, and my sins, and the very reason that prompted me to join the lodge urged me to forsake it."

But does the Scripture not say, "Other foundation can no man lay than that is laid, which is Jesus Christ." This being so, have we any right to bind ourselves by oath to an order from which His sacred Name is excluded? If we truly love Him, will we frequent any place where we must leave Him outside the door?

Our Attitude

If what is written above can be substantiated, and we believe it can, the attitude of the Christian who recognizes the authority of Scripture is not difficult to determine. Hear the Word of God:

"Have no fellowship with the unfruitful works of darkness, but rather reprove them" (Eph. 5: 11).

There are some who say they are strong enough to resist any adverse influence of the lodge. Perhaps they are strong, but to such St. Paul gives a relevant admonition.

"Take heed lest by any means this liberty of yours become a stumbling-block to them that are weak. . . . Wherefore if meat make my brother to offend, I will eat no flesh while the world standeth, lest I make my brother to offend" (1 Cor. 8: 9–13).

To the Mason whose conscience is uneasy on account of some feature of the lodge, these words give helpful counsel:

"Now we command you, brethren, in the name of our Lord Jesus Christ, that ye withdraw yourselves from every brother that walketh disorderly and not after the tradition which he received of us" (2 Thess. 3: 6).

The final and inescapable word is spoken by St. Paul:

"Be ye not unequally yoked together with unbelievers: For what fellowship hath righteousness with unrighteousness? And what communion hath light with darkness? And what concord hath Christ with Belial? Or what part hath he that believeth with an infidel? And what agreement hath the Temple of God with idols? For ye are the temple of the Living God; as God hath said, I will dwell in them and walk in them; and I will be their God, and they shall be my people. Wherefore come ye out from among them, and be ye separate saith the Lord, and touch not the unclean thing; and I will receive you. And I will be a father unto you, and ye shall be my sons and daughters, saith the Lord Almighty" (2 Cor. 6: 14–18).

We close with the words of the late Dwight L. Moody spoken in this connection:

"I do not see how any Christian, most of all a Christian minister, can go into these secret lodges with unbelievers. They say they have more influence for good, but I say they can have more influence for good by staying out of them, and then reproving their evil deeds. Abraham had more influence for good in Sodom than Lot had. If twenty-five Christians go into a secret lodge with fifty who are not Christians, the fifty can vote anything they please, and the twenty-five will be partakers of their sins. They are unequally yoked with unbelievers."

XIV

THE HEALING MOVEMENT

IN a world racked with suffering, it is little wonder that great interest is being displayed in what is popularly termed "faith healing." The Bible itself has much to say on the subject. If Divine healing is universally available through the atonement of Christ, as many are teaching, then the Church is criminally guilty if she withholds these glad tidings from suffering humanity. If, on the other hand, healing is not thus universally available, then those who encourage such a belief are guilty of callous and cruel deception.

In his most sane and helpful book,[1] H. W. Frost writes in this connection: "If a believer holds something to be a privilege which God has never provided as such, the non-attainment of it must necessarily produce reaction, with disastrous results. Such an experience will mean that the man of God will conclude, either that God for some reason has forsaken him, or that he himself in some particular has forsaken God, when as a matter of fact neither the one nor the other may be true.

"I have seen many such cases in connection with the doctrine of miraculous healing, some of which have been unspeakably sad, where, because of the holding of an unscriptural and unworkable theory, the saint in spite of a complete life-consecration, was living in the darkness of despondency, amounting in some cases to despair. The only correction of such an experience is to come down from the unwarranted position which has been assumed, to solid Scripture ground, and there to abide. Such a course may not make for a sense of peculiarity or for an extra reputation of sanctity; but it will certainly lead to heart-rest and a true testimony before God and man."

[1] H. W. Frost, *Miraculous Healing.*

DIVINE HEALING TAUGHT

From personal experience as well as from observation and investigation, the writer is convinced of the possibility of Divine healing, both with and without external means. Well-authenticated cases with which he is familiar have convinced him of the undiminished efficacy of Christ's healing touch, and preclude a hostile approach to the subject. There are, however, certain features of modern healing movements which require challenge.

First, let us briefly set out the Scripture teaching on the subject.

Old Testament

Early in Israel's history, God revealed Himself thus: "I am the Lord that healeth thee" (Exod. 15 : 26). But even then His promise of healing was not unconditional. "If thou wilt keep all the statutes, I will put none of these diseases upon thee," was the word. His statutes embodied many health laws which are advocated today and which were designed to ensure their national health. It is entirely gratuitous to assume that the reference here is to miraculous healing. In his excellent book,[1] the late Dr. R. V. Bingham enumerates six of the laws: *Sanitation*, preventing infection (Deut. 23 : 14); *Sterilization*, guarding against contagion (Lev. 11 : 32, 39, 40); *Quarantine*, isolating infectious diseases (Num. 5 : 4; 31 : 22, 23); *Hygiene and Dietetics* (Lev. 11; 19 : 7; Num. 11 : 19, 20); *Physical Culture*; each Israelite, even the priest, worked his own lot (Deut. 16 : 16); *Recuperation*, the seventh day and the seventh month reserved for rest. Faithful observance of these laws, even in our day, would in very many cases dispense with the necessity for miraculous intervention.

It is to be noted that it was God who permitted Satan to afflict Job with disease, and that not because of his sin, but because of his integrity! (Job 1 : 6–21; 2 : 1–10). Perhaps it would be appropriate to make passing reference to Ps. 103 : 3, "Who healeth all thy diseases." This is taken as referring to physical healing, but the Psalmist is careful to state that he is addressing his soul, not his body. The soul has its diseases as well as the body. And can the following verse, "Thy youth is renewed like the eagle's," be referred to the body? To be

---

[1] *The Bible and the Body.*

consistent, it must refer to the renewing of the physical youth.

New Testament

The outstandingly clear New Testament passage is Jas. 5: 14–18. From it we learn: (*a*) The sick man is to take the initiative, and call for the elders. (*b*) The elders are to anoint the sufferer (apparently implying dedication and surrender), and to pray over him. (*c*) The prayer of faith of the elders saves the sufferer. "Faith is the gift of God, given when it is His will to answer that particular prayer in that particular way. We have to fulfil certain conditions ourselves to obtain this gift of faith, but it is not granted if the prayer for healing is not in accordance with the will of God. It is only too easy for true faith to be counterfeited by fatuous optimism."[1]

Here in brief are some of the main New Testament teachings:

(*a*) The unchanging God does heal today, but nowhere does Scripture assert that He always wills to heal everyone.

(*b*) The use of means, or consulting a doctor is not prohibited by God (2 Kings 20: 7; Isa. 37: 21; John 9: 6–11; Acts 19: 11, 12; 1 Tim. 5: 23; Matt. 9: 12). In the ultimate, all healing whether with or without means, is Divine healing.

(*c*) The healings of Scripture contrary to most present-day healings, were instantaneous, not gradual, e.g. Mark 1: 42; complete, not partial, e.g. Matt. 8: 15; permanent, not temporary, e.g. Luke 7: 15.

(*d*) The Divine sovereignty is exercised in the healing of His creatures. With two exceptions, Christ healed only Jews. The twelve and seventy were forbidden to heal any but Jews (Matt. 10: 5–8). There were cases which God did not choose to heal (Phil. 2: 25–30; 1 Tim. 5: 23; 2 Tim. 4: 20). There was one case He refused to heal (2 Cor. 12: 7–10).

(*e*) God delivers in sickness either by removing it, or by strengthening to bear it (1 Cor. 10: 13; 2 Cor. 12: 9).

(*f*) Christ did not always require faith on the part of the sufferer (Matt. 9: 32; Mark 7: 35; Luke 22: 51). In fact in only one case out of every four recorded, was personal faith present. Nor did He confine His ministry to believers, as do many healers today (Matt. 4: 24; 8: 16). Need, not faith, commanded His healing touch.

[1] A. R. Short, *Bible and Modern Science*, p. 125.

(g) While the God Who controls the laws of the universe can modify or suspend these at His will, it seems to be His method not to employ supernatural means when natural means will effect the desired result. It is not a question of what God *can* do, but what He is *pleased* to do.

(h) Amazingly enough, there is only one recorded case of a Christian being healed—Paul himself—and his was no ordinary case of blindness (Acts 9: 18).

DIVINE HEALING TRAVESTIED

Faith-healing movements are by no means modern developments. There have always been those who are ready to profit by the misfortunes of others, and to exploit one of the devil's few true assertions: "All that a man hath will he give for his life" (Job 2: 4). In saying this, we do not imply that all who teach healing by faith are charlatans.

Modern healers have a flying start with their propaganda, since it is an established medical fact that seventy-five per cent of sick people recover normally, through Nature's healing agency alone. Psychotherapy, or the power of the mind over bodily functions, is being increasingly employed by doctors. But long ago the medicine-men of pagan tribes used this knowledge to their own advantage. Dr. J. L. Nevius of Korea asserts that miraculous healing and speaking in tongues are practised today in absolutely heathen circles.

In the last century, Edward Irving gave fresh impetus to the healing movement. *Mormonism* early adopted healing as one of its planks, and proclaims many miracles. *Spiritism* boasts of its spirit-healings. *Christian Science* claims to have "discovered the science of metaphysical healing." *New Thought* was brought to the birth on its "Phrenopathic method of cure." *Roman Catholicism* makes much of miraculous cures through relics and pilgrimages to Lourdes, etc. *Unity* teaches "Christian healing."

On the other hand, to be perfectly fair, there have been many saintly men and women who have, with more sanity and restraint, been ardent advocates of Divine healing. Among them were Dr. A. J. Gordon, Dr. A. B. Simpson and Dr. Andrew Murray, each of whom wrote books on the subject. The association of these honoured names with the movement has unfortunately identified them with much from which they would have vigorously dissociated themselves.

But in this connection it is not out of place to record the fact that Drs. A. J. Gordon and A. B. Simpson, although both had previously experienced remarkable healings, at last succumbed to diseases from which they were not cured, Dr. Gordon died from bronchitis and pneumonia, and Dr. Simpson from arterio-sclerosis. Although much prayer was offered for each of them by those who believed earnestly in Divine healing, such healing was not vouchsafed, and they passed away in suffering. Dr. Andrew Murray, too, fell ill towards the close of his life of the sickness from which he died, and resorted to medical aid. His attitude, as one would expect, was one of submission to the will of God. "My child," he said to his daughter, "I would so much like to hold evangelistic meetings, but God does not see fit to heal me."

One question which demands an answer before it can be asserted that healing is a universal boon, has to do with the incidence of sickness.

Is All Sickness of the Devil?

Sickness is the result of sin, for had there been no sin, there would have been neither sickness nor death. In this sense, sickness may be said to be of the devil. But it is quite another thing to say that sickness is always the result of personal or hereditary sin. When the disciples of our Lord inquired of Him as to the cause of the blindness of the man in John 9, they said, "Who did sin, this man or his parents that he was born blind?" Jesus answered, "Neither hath this man sinned, nor his parents, *but that the works of God should be made manifest in him.*"

It is true that some sicknesses were recognised by our Lord as coming from the devil, e.g., Luke 13: 16; Acts 10: 38; but the Bible also teaches that sickness is inflicted by God, as e.g., the leprosy of Miriam, Uzziah and Gehazi. As has already been remarked, Job's affliction was specifically the outcome of his piety, not of his sin, and it issued in the greater glory of God. It can with equal assurance be affirmed that Hudson Taylor's long-standing heart trouble was not associated with sin, since both the inception and the development of the great China Inland Mission synchronised with his physical breakdowns. As Dr. Lockyer comments, "Dr. Taylor's times of physical weakness were not times of spiritual declension, but contrariwise, they were commonly the times of closest communion with Christ."

"Many of God's servants have suffered many years of ill-health and many have died young. We think of John Calvin, David Brainerd, Frances Ridley Havergal, Robert Murray McCheyne, Charles Haddon Spurgeon and Fanny Crosby, to name only a few. . . . We must conclude that spiritual health or 'wholeness' is no guarantee at all of physical well-being; and certainly physical health is no measure of one's spiritual condition."[1]

The great healing campaigns of today are entirely without New Testament precedent or parallel. The common procedure is for applicants for healing to be "weeded out" and classified. Usually, Christians alone are healed and faith is regarded as essential on their part. If healing does not ensue, the failure is usually attributed to their lack of faith. When our Lord and the apostles healed, there were no disillusioned and disappointed crowds of sufferers turned back uncured and embittered against Christianity as is the case today. In one healing service in America conducted by a celebrated healer, only forty out of seven hundred people were selected to be healed. Many of the healers are the very antithesis of the Great Physician who repeatedly avoided publicity and refused to conduct a campaign of self-advertisement (Mark 1: 23–29).

The keystone of the whole system is that healing is in the atonement.

Is Healing in the Atonement?

The key verse of this theory is Matt. 8: 17, "Himself took our infirmities and bore our diseases." This verse is practically the sole warrant for such an assertion. Strange indeed it is, that in not one Epistle is there even a hint that there is healing for us in the atonement. All the apostles unite in declaring that Christ atoned for our *sins* on the cross, but none affirms that He atoned for our *sicknesses*. See Rom. 3: 25; 5: 6–11; 2 Cor. 5: 18–21; 1 Pet. 2: 24.

[1] A. C. Hill, *Divine Healing Examined by a Physician.*

Mrs. Aimée Semple McPherson taught that our healing was purchased at the whipping-post, where "by His stripes we are healed." Her words are, "At the whipping-post He purchased your healing"—thus teaching that there were two atonements, one by the lash and the other by the blood-shedding.

There is no scriptural basis for the claim of one healing group that "through the merits of Christ's atoning work on Calvary, the curse of sin and disease was removed once and for all", nor for the assertion that "Since Christ bore the sins of the whole world, and the sickness, man is not punished *for* his sins; man is punished *by* his sins. God could not punish mankind for something He has removed for ever through the death of His Son." The argument sounds convincing, but how does it tally with Rev. 20: 13–15? "They were judged every man according to his works . . . and whosoever was not found written in the book of life was cast into the lake of fire." That certainly sounds as though they are punished *for* their sins.

IMPLICATIONS OF THIS TEACHING

Let us consider what is involved in the doctrine that healing is in the atonement for all.

1. All sick saints are so because of sin, or being out of communion with God. But what shall we say of children who are sick? Are they so because of sin?

2. It takes away comfort from the sick-bed, and brands the sufferer with unbelief or positive wrongdoing. The invalid is so because of sin.

3. The use of medicine or other means, or the calling of a doctor is an affront to God.

4. If disease is atoned for as well as sin, then healing would be as eternal as salvation, and death would be impossible.

5. The atonement must be a failure, for everyone dies, and most become sick and die.

We confidently affirm that nowhere does Scripture assert that sickness requires atonement, or that sickness is always or necessarily the result of sin. Sin was the only thing demanding expiation by blood. Let sufferers who are confused on this issue, take all the comfort they can out of our Lord's statement in John 9: 2, 3. Nor does Scripture encourage us to believe that the atonement does away with the temporal effects of sin (Rom. 8: 19–23).

Four Awkward Cases

Proponents of the healing-in-atonement theory have some awkward cases to explain away.

Epaphroditus (Phil. 2: 27). Was his sickness the result of his sin? See Phil. 2: 30. Why did Paul who possessed the gift of healing not heal him?

Trophimus (2 Tim. 4: 20). Why did not Paul, instead of leaving him sick, urge him to claim his healing through the atonement?

Timothy (1 Tim. 5: 23). Was Timothy out of touch with God? Why did not Paul pray the prayer of faith, instead of prescribing a medical remedy?

Paul (2 Cor. 12: 7; Gal 4: 13, 14). Healers maintain that Paul's "thorn in the flesh" was not sickness, but the evidence is all to the contrary. Paul speaks of "the infirmity of the flesh." It is the body which becomes infirm, not the soul. Was Paul ignorant that healing was in the atonement? The denial of healing by God only served to cause Paul to glory in his infirmity, that the power of Christ might rest upon him.

Isaiah's Prophecy

If Matt. 8: 17 and Isa. 53: 4 do not teach that healing is in the atonement, what is their significance?

The word for "griefs" or "disease," though often signifying physical disease is also used to signify soul-sickness (Jer. 6: 7; 10: 19; Isa. 17: 11). The word for "sorrows" or "pains," almost always signifies soul-distress (Isa. 65: 14; Ps. 32: 10, etc.). If Isa. 53: 4 is read in its context it will be seen beyond doubt that it is sickness of the soul the prophet has in view— iniquities, transgressions, sins. The figure of sickness is used consistently throughout Isaiah's prophecy, as referring to a sinful condition. Peter's quotation of the same passage refers it to sin, and not a word is said about sickness (1 Pet. 2: 24). It is our sins which are healed by His stripes, not our sicknesses.

Further, it is to be noted that Matthew expressly says that this prophecy was fulfilled then and there, before Christ came to the Cross, in His early lifetime. Dr. Bingham points out that "Matthew deliberately drops the substitutionary word for 'bear' which Isaiah uses, and uses another word for 'bear' which is never associated with propitiation or atonement. Who authorized Matthew to make such a change unless he was guided by the Holy Spirit? . . . The word is used in Gal. 6: 2 to express sympathetic bearing, as also in Rom. 15: 1."

We conclude therefore, that that portion of Isaiah's prophecy as quoted by Matthew, was fulfilled by Christ bearing sympathetically in his spirit, during His lifetime, the infirmities and pains of those He healed. He entered into the suffering and sorrows of those He healed, as witnessed by the statement, "He perceived that virtue had gone out of Him." "In all their afflictions He was afflicted," He was "touched with the feeling of our infirmities."

We firmly believe that there is healing for the believer, within the limits of the will of God, but we base our belief on other Scriptures than these. There is no Scriptural precedent or warrant for the present-day healing services in which autosuggestion and hypnotic influences play such a large part, and are frequently followed by bleak disillusionment.

Two well-qualified Christian medical men who made a special investigation of the subject of faith healing, while freely admitting the possibility of an abnormal response by God to the prayers of His people, had this to say as a result of their research. "The fact is that, from an examination of the results of the work of faith healers and of healing missions which are recorded in current writings, the impression is gained that little which can be said to be truly miraculous occurs today. Disappointing as it may seem, the facts do not warrant the rather sweeping assertions and self-advertisement of many of the healing practitioners.

"After considering evidence from a widely distributed number of sources, the special committee of the British Medical Association sums up its findings in the following words:[1]

"'We can find no evidence that there is any type of illness cured by "spiritual healing" alone which could not have been

[1] *Divine Healing and Co-operation Between Doctors and Clergy*, p. 15.

cured by medical treatment which necessarily includes consideration of environmental factors. We find that, whilst patients suffering from psychogenic disorders may be "cured" by various methods of spiritual healing, just as they are by methods of suggestion and other forms of psychological treatment employed by doctors, we can find no evidence that organic diseases are cured solely by such means. The evidence suggests that many such cases claimed to be cured are likely to be either instances of wrong diagnosis, wrong prognosis, remission or possibly of spontaneous cure.'

"This last phrase 'spontaneous cure' was taken up by one section of the press, as begging the whole question, but medical observers are constantly made aware of such 'spontaneous' recoveries, remissions or regressions in cases where there were no known spiritual influences at work."[1]

Further interesting facts emerged from their study. There seems to be no appreciable difference in the vital statistics and longevity of the members of healing movements or among Christian Scientists as compared with those of the general population. The impression was gained that a comparison of the figures for "spontaneous" cures and those attributed to faith healing was insignificant. The small residuum of cases in which, on the evidence of the faith healers, there had been recovery from "malignant growths," did not appear to differ much from the rare cases of spontaneous regression in general practice, where no religious influence was claimed. They found—as have many other investigators—that by far the majority of cures were of certain functional conditions common in the neurological and psychiatric departments of a hospital and which are today being treated successfully by ordinary methods.

A final word of warning should be added. *God is not the only healer*, and therefore the fact of a healing is not necessarily evidence of the activity of God. The prophetic Scriptures clearly foretell that the closing days of this age will be characterised by a revival of supernatural phenomena. 2 Thess. 2: 9, 10 speaks of the advent of one "whose coming is after the working of Satan with all power and signs and lying wonders, and with all deceivableness of unrighteousness." Our Lord warned that "there shall arise false Christs, and false prophets, and shall shew great signs and wonders; insomuch

[1] Edmunds and Scorer, *Some Thoughts on Faith Healing*, p. 54.

that, *if it were possible, they shall deceive the very elect.* Behold I have told you before" (Matt. 24: 24, 25). Let us be alert to apply the test of the Word of God to every movement which specialises in the miraculous (I Tim. 4: 1; I John 4: 1, 2).

XV

BRIEF SUMMARY OF OTHER CULTS

ANTHROPOSOPHY

Founded by Rudolf Steiner, an Austrian intellectual who was born in 1861 and died in 1925. Once a lecturer with the Theosophical Society, he broke away in 1913 as a result of growing disagreement with their tenets. The movement he fathered has some kinship with the western esotericism of the Rosicrucians. To Steiner, Christ is not one of many Saviours, nor the product of many reincarnations, but he reproduces the Nestorian error of differentiating between the Christ and Jesus. At the baptism, the Son of God descended on the Son of Man. The atonement of Christ is not viewed as substitutionary, but through His death Christ defeated the powers of evil and made it possible for man to rise into new life. The law of Karma and reincarnation as in Theosophy form part of his teaching.

BAHA'I

Claims to be the universal religion. This Persian religion had three Persian leaders. The first, known as The Bab (The Gate) proclaimed himself in 1844 as the Mahdi, the promised messenger foretold by Mohammed. Next came Baha'u'llah (The Glory of God) who in 1863 declared that he was the one foretold by The Bab, whom God had chosen to inaugurate a new era in a world in which the Fatherhood of God and the brotherhood of man would become a reality. The third was 'Abdul-Baha (The Servant of the Glory) who was son of Baha'u'llah and died in 1921.

The Baha'i faith has no positive doctrine of sin, atonement or forgiveness. There is progress after death, but no reincarnation. All religions are the manifestation of God and embodiments of the Holy Spirit, and none are superior to the others. Christ is merely one of the nine great religious teachers of the world.

COONEYITES

Founded by W. W. Irvine in Ireland in 1897. Later Edward Cooney headed the movement and greatly developed it. Its adherents disown the name "Cooneyite," and it is difficult to induce them to disclose their affiliation. They go forth by twos, practise austerity of dress and living, and achieve their greatest success in country areas. Church buildings are anathema and meetings are held in homes or tents. Conversion to the "Jesus Way" is essential to salvation, as also is baptism by immersion administered by one of their preachers, and breaking of all ecclesiastical ties. Conversion is possible only in their meetings and through their preachers. They have no literature. Marriage is often discouraged and frequently existing marriages are broken. As to doctrine, they deny the sinlessness of Christ and His vicarious atonement. Salvation is through imitating the life of Jesus.

I AM CULT

A modification of Yogi or Hindu mysticism. Man ascends above the physical to a spiritual plane where all dross is removed, through attainment of higher human virtue. Eventually he may attain perfection and eternal life and ascend without death through a cycle of reincarnations. He then returns to earth as one of the Ascended Masters to assist others who are ascending. Jesus is now on earth in spirit and has delegated to St. Germaine the throne of authority. Bible teaching is discouraged—it should be renounced and forgotten. Prayer and adoration are to be offered to St. Germaine as supreme spiritual ruler. Demonic influence is manifest in the movement.

NEW THOUGHT

Has close ties with Christian Science and shares its pantheism. This cult which had its origin with Warren Felt Evans, has no creed or dogma and ignores the Biblical doctrines of sin and salvation. God is spirit and spirit is principle. Sin, sickness and death can be overcome through the introduction of true thought into the mind of man, for everything is only a thought. It affirms the supremacy of mind over matter and the possibility of curing disease by purely mental means.

Christ was not the only great Prophet of God and the Holy Spirit is ignored. Being created in the perfect image and likeness of God, man is God incarnate. Evil and the devil are non-existent.

ROSICRUCIANISM (The Rose Cross)

The order of Rosicrucians was founded by Christian Rosenkreuz who lived in the thirteenth century. Its modern apostle was the late Max Heindel. Adherents see in the cross, not an emblem of suffering and shame, but a symbol of "the life currents vitalizing the bodies of plants, animals and man." They have an elaborate mystic explanation of this symbolism. The common greeting is, "May roses bloom on your cross" with the response, "And on yours also." There are many points of similarity with Theosophy. To the Rosicrucian there are seven worlds, not separated by space or distance but by rate of vibration. Each of these worlds, as well as man, passes through seven Periods of Rebirths. The World of Thought which consists of seven regions, has two main divisions—concrete and abstract. There are three heavens through which man progresses. Christ is not the only begotten Son of God, which teaching is stigmatized as "a great mistake." He repeatedly returns to earth and offers an annual sacrifice. "Christ is imprisoned in the most literal sense of the word from Christmas to Easter." Man is divine as his Father in heaven.

SWEDENBORGIANISM

Founded by the Swedish scientist and philosopher, Emanuel Swedenborg, a man possessed of remarkable psychic gifts who saw visions and believed he received revelations from God. His method of treating the Scriptures enabled him to import into the words a meaning suited to his own philosophy. The orthodox doctrine of the Trinity is denied. Christ inherited evil from His mother. The personality of Satan is denied. Christ's death was not vicarious and Paul's doctrine of the imputation of righteousness is disallowed. There is no resurrection.